When Home Wasn't Enough

Douglas Schnapp

Copyright © 2025 Douglas Schnapp

All rights reserved

No part of this book may be reproduced, or stored in a retrieval system, or transmitted in any form or by any means, electronic, mechanical, photocopying, recording, or otherwise, without express written permission of the publisher.

ISBN: 979-8-9891218-8-5

Cover design by: Douglas Schnapp

Prologue

I was thirty-six years old in 2016 when my second marriage ended. My second house with a white picket fence in suburbia was empty aside from me. Long-term committed relationships had consumed the previous fifteen years of my life. From the time my second marriage ended in 2016 to around that same time a year later, I remained away from the online meetup and hookup sites as I focused on finding myself.

Career was a stressful and unfulfilling endeavor. I resented my career; all the time and effort I put forth to exhaust myself thanklessly. I couldn't feel good about myself as I traded time for money. One of those in trade was not a renewable resource. I felt shorter changed than ever.

By the time I was in my late thirties, I was vacant. I was bored. I was burnt out. A few encumbrances kept me loosely tethered and grounded in northwest Ohio. A mental break and midlife crisis were inevitable. I was lost and alone, a feeling that carried with me my entire life, a broken shell of a person, but that shell shined and glimmered to anyone on the outside looking in…as long as they didn't look too closely.

I reached to the online world as a new direction and experience to feel something out of life. Until late 2017, the rise and progression of both the internet and social networking had gone along in a universe separate from my own. I joined the website in the winter of 2017, around the holidays. That website was my very first foray into the world of online adult meeting and hookup culture. Though I was brand new, I came across many other users who had been active on the site for a full decade prior. I had much to learn.

By the end of 2017, I had created thousands of media items; pictures, videos, full-length movies, etc. Over ten thousand of those were screenshots from comments, direct messages, and conversations from just the one specific website; a network of connected adult social platforms boasting forty million active worldwide users on six continents.

My approach to making my profile had worked quickly. Having fresh eyes with no bias allowed me to stand out in a sea of generic and boring clones. My approach catapulted me to the forefront of the website, and I wasn't ready. I began making money on the site instantly. I began interacting with people from all over the world. I began live-streaming to an audience which grew anytime I turned on the live camera.

By spring of 2018, I had my new routine down. Days were spent with my new power tools and supplies, working in my driveway. I was learning and installing car audio. The best sound, the most bass, the perfect balance; I loved my new obsession. Crystal meth kept me hyper focused. When friends stopped by, I excitedly showed them and explained what I had done to create such sound.

Indoors, I began teaching myself video editing, producing, and creating on the laptop I bought in January with the software I had been buying since then. I very much enjoyed making custom videos and sharing interactions with others online. Crystal meth fueled my hypersexuality. Most days, I spent an hour working out. I also went tanning daily. Both activities gave me more opportunities to fulfill specific intimate video requests. Most of my time was spent interacting with new romantic interests, both online and in the real world.

In the evenings, with a concert playing in the background on my living room television, my interactions amplified. By spring of 2018, I had been meeting people from the internet for months. Sometimes we went for coffee, other times we went to a park or to get some food. Sometimes intimate partners would stop over. Other times, I would just pick them up and bring them back to my house. Long nights and sometimes full weekends of beautiful and abstract intimacy were standard. Unencumbered and free interactions, connections allowing fantasies and experimentation were fostered in open and honest communication; no judgement, no embarrassment, just passion.

All of life changed for me in 2018. Beyond newfound online popularity, another darker world had already consumed me. I had a master-key to a new kingdom; one that would fuel my endeavors in the coming years. I was soon fully immersed in that strange new scene like a kid in a candy store. Steroids, street drugs, prescriptions; all were just a call away. The line between caution and paranoia was ever so slightly there. I focused on being careful and thorough, but as with the new online world, there were blind corners I could only see once I looked back at them.

Those two new worlds left no room for the life I had pseudo-built and rebuilt the entire time I had been alive: the home and career, the interactions of my daily universe, friends, relationships, family, location, everything familiar to me over the decades up to that point. I had dreamed of letting go of all I knew. I wanted freedom from work. I wanted to travel. I wanted to feel alive. As I felt my career winding down, my desire to travel consumed me. As my internet popularity grew, opportunities arose. In an illicit substance market, I embraced a new source of income. I was ready to step from the edge.

All the circumstances lined up. It was time to leave everything else in the past. I needed to feel alive. For thirty-eight years, I had chased happiness. In all those years, I just couldn't seem to find it. I had been doing it wrong. It was time to see what else was out there beyond northwest Ohio. 2018 was set to be the year when I truly began to live. I gave myself no other option.

DOUGLAS SCHNAPP

Drugs aren't the problem.

Drugs aren't the solution.

When Home Wasn't Enough

DOUGLAS SCHNAPP

A Perfect Storm

I had been awake for days. I was dirty, I was sweaty, I was greasy, and I was expecting the call and a subsequent break from my obsessive car stereo installation. A full day had been spent in my driveway with my power tools, working on yet more speakers for my car stereo system. The sunlight began to fade in the early evening. Clouds began to roll in. I stepped back inside. From my kitchen, I returned messages, interacted with online intimate partners, and consumed more crystal. Although my meth consumption could have fueled additional work outdoors, the rain had begun its protest.

Angie's text messages that evening were frequent and impatient. I could have acquiesced, but it was a matter of principle. I decided, due to her annoying pestering, my last couple of ounces were not going anywhere until I reupped. Angie abandoned texting, and she called me as I waited for the other phone call.

"Dude, I told you…I'm gonna get the call this evening. I'm going back outside to try to finish this last speaker before the storm hits."

"It's just my friends up North are getting…"

"Hang on. That's the call on my other line."

"Hello, Angie? Yeah, that was him. I'm rolling up there now. I'll hit you up once I get back."

My car was a disaster. There were bolts, screws, cut wires, and tools all over the place. I left it the way it was. The sun was setting as the rain began to fall. It was a good stopping point that evening. I was exhausted after twenty-four hours of nonstop car audio work. I washed my hands but didn't bother to shower or change out of my dirty clothes.

On the return trip, the clouds had become an off-and-on thundershower. Construction on the bridge over the river from Toledo had been constant in northwest Ohio for some time. Orange barrels continued as I drove south, past the casino in Rossford, and towards the first of the Perrysburg freeway exits. The speed limit changed often. The highway was under constant repair, and state troopers almost always sat in pairs in the median between the northbound and southbound traffic lanes.

The two cruisers were perched like hawks at the break in the median just south of the last Rossford exit overpass. I saw them well before I passed them with the flow of traffic in the rain that night. The posted speed on that particular stretch of road, due to the ever-present roadwork, was sixty miles-per-hour. I saw the sign as clearly as I had seen the speed trap. It was nothing new.

I continued to drive with the flow of traffic. As a reflex, I glanced at the speedometer. I was traveling at sixty-four miles-per-hour. The rain was coming down hard. My acknowledgement of the police was fleeting. I was far more concerned with choosing which of the Perrysburg exits to use to get home. I had just minutes to go, regardless of which exit I decided to take. Traffic was in a tight pattern, and I was in the passing lane to the far left. I'd need to cross four lanes rather quickly if I wished to use that first exit. I decided that exit was my preference.

Just as I was about to switch lanes in front of another car to cross over to my preferred Perrysburg exit, all of my mirrors lit up with blue and red flashing lights. I couldn't believe I hadn't noticed the police officer behind me. With no ticket history and a habit of driving with my head on a swivel, I always adhered closely to posted signage and speed limits. I thought I had been doing so that evening.

I had a manilla envelope, stuffed to the brim, riding shotgun with me in full view from any angle in the front passenger seat. My startled brain irrationally pictured drug dogs, but only for a second. It was a traffic stop, not a drug search. I used my turn signal when I crossed the four lanes of traffic and pulled to a stop on the right shoulder. I was a hundred yards shy of that coveted first Perrysburg exit.

The rain suddenly stopped with the car. I turned on the dome light as I cracked my window. I hadn't thought it through. The officer didn't walk up to my window. Instead, I was surprised by a flashlight shining into the passenger side of my car, the side with the fully stuffed envelope.

I pushed the button to roll down the passenger side window. By that point, the officer's light had flashed directly onto my weekly supply of methamphetamine. As with the scattered stereo equipment and tools, the flashlight didn't stay on the envelope each time it lit it up. I stayed calm. The officer made a request; he asked me to step out of the car.

The officer patted me down as I stood on the shoulder of the highway. He then directed me to sit in the police car while he ran my information. I had already handed over my license before I stepped from my car, which was fortunate since my wallet had fallen onto the seat as I exited. It would have been a potential situation had the officer needed to search for it while I sat in the cruiser and watched.

"So, I pulled you over for speeding…"

I had been speeding, just not in the way the officer thought.

"I didn't think I was over the speed limit."

"Why were you so close to the car in front of you?"

"I made a last minute decision to get off at this exit. I needed to get up past that other car."

"Well, I'm not gonna give you a ticket for speeding, but since I already called it in, I have to give you a ticket for assured clear distance."

I left with a ticket for one hundred and twenty dollars. I was not pleased with my first ticket in many years, but I was relieved I was free to walk back to my car.

The five-minute remainder of the drive home on the surface streets of Perrysburg seemed to take forever. I was alone on the quiet suburban streets. I kept my car stereo off; no need to draw anymore unwanted attention. As I pulled into my driveway, I grabbed my package from the front seat. A few short steps, and then I was safe. I breathed a sigh of relief once I was inside, and I quickly locked my front door.

After I texted Angie, I went ahead and tested the new shipment. As always, it was of purity unmatched. Angie showed up, and I told her the story of my drive home. I then gave her the boot rather quickly. I had other plans that night.

At that point, I had been awake the entire previous week. I closed the door behind Angie and locked it again. I then walked through my home and my garage. I made sure all the other doors and windows were locked.

I made sure the house was in order, and I turned off all the lights and electronics. I filled a large glass with water and set it on the nightstand next to my bed. Once my phone was shut off, I sat down on my mattress. It was time to rest. I took five of my two-milligram Klonopins with one sip of water and called it a week.

A thought crossed my mind before the drugs hit. My mind drifted a decade back, to the night before my mom passed away after seventeen years of cancer. That last conversation I had with her replayed as vividly as if it had just taken place. My mom's words echoed in my thoughts.

"I'm ready to go. I'm just not ready to leave you."

"Go ahead and go. You deserve to be free of the pain. You've done more for me than I ever could have hoped. You'll always be with me. I'll be okay."

My last words to her, they replayed in my head as the benzos began to take hold and overpower the crystal. I had been trying to be okay ever since. I wondered if I would ever make good on that last promise. I closed my eyes. It was a Friday night when I went to bed. I woke up the following Tuesday afternoon.

Mow Money, Mow Problems

I had just finished mowing my front lawn for the third time. By early June, I was already far behind schedule on my mowing duties. As if on cue, my riding mower coughed its last bit from the exhaust, backfired, and the engine cut off completely. I pushed the mower up my driveway, along the side of my house, and into the pole barn out back.

Sweat dripped from my body, and I was breathing heavily. I stepped out to the pavement as the overhead door closed behind me. The front yard was in order, but the grass in my back yard was a jungle. It came up well above my waist in most places. I shook my head and smiled as I stood there in front of my barn and surveyed the wilderness that was my back yard.

During the spring of 2018, I had only mowed the front yard three times, deliberately avoiding the back yard because of the added difficulty. I also knew the riding mower was on its last year in operating condition. My back yard was enclosed by a seven-foot wooden privacy fence, stretching from the sides of my house to the far back. In the far back, a line of trees, bushes, and plants completely shielded my yard from the neighbors on the next block over.

As I was looking through my mail one afternoon, I came across a letter from the city. The letter immediately delayed all of my upcoming travel plans. The letter caused me a massive stress headache the rest of that week, and it sparked the first battle in a war which wouldn't end until a full half year later, both sides taking heavy losses. A medical emergency in fall, resulting from the mower conflict, would be like no injury I had ever experienced...but that was still months away.

No longer working since May 18th of 2018, I was finalizing ideas to begin a summer of extensive travel. I had people to meet, places to see, drugs to consume, and a mind I was looking to escape.

It was a Tuesday when the letter came. Until I read it, I had planned to leave to begin the summer of travel with a trip to see a trans lady down in Kentucky. For the second time within a couple of weeks, I had to let the lady know that the visit needed to be pushed back.

The letter from the city was blunt and to the point. If I didn't mow my back yard by that upcoming Friday, I was going to be fined six hundred dollars and charged a rate of seventy-five dollars an hour for city workers to complete the job themselves. Did the one neighbor with a view of my yard complain to the city? Had the new city property auditor overstepped his bounds by peeking over my fence into my back yard? It didn't matter at that point. What mattered then was putting in the work before the deadline.

I called all kinds of mowing and landscaping services. Some companies explained that I was out of their range of coverage. Others were at full client capacity for the year. Still others were not taking on new clients in the immediate future, with two weeks being the soonest anyone could make it to the house.

Late that night, my tweaked and stressed brain formulated an idea. I spent four hours outside with a machete and a flashlight. The next morning, I knew that it had been wasted time. I had an acre of lawn, three quarters of it was the back yard. The grass was thick and tall. The amount I had handled with a machete emphasized how I needed an actual mower.

With a tweaked and stressed brain, I set my sights on fixing the dead riding mower that Wednesday. I had two more days, and I had confidence in my abilities. Whether it was false confidence or not was yet to be seen.

In the time since I had left the corporate world just a few weeks prior, I had bought new tools from a hardware store. I had previously changed a starter in one of my cars as well as two alternators. I had installed an intricately self-built a complicated car audio system. I had changed car batteries. In one of my cars, I rewired the electrical system under the hood. Though learning by myself as I made those changes and upgrades had been challenging, all was eventually completed successfully.

As the sun went down that Friday evening, I was happy I had finished the repairs to the mower six hours before it grew dark that night. I hadn't anticipated the two extra hours of hardship once the mowing began. The grass was beyond thick and tall. It towered above the tractor as I rode on it and mowed. Especially out in the back third, the lawn almost swallowed the mower...and me right along with it.

The deck of the tractor, which held the blades, was raised as high as it could go. The motor labored to keep the blades spinning, often stalling out completely. It was slow going. Deep gashes on my fingers from the repair job began to bleed anytime the mower jerked as I tried to keep the steering wheel steady.

One of the rear tires had completely blown and slid down off the wheel hub an hour into the mowing, leaving it completely flat and useless. The next five hours of bouncing made me wish for relief for my tailbone. My arm and shoulder muscles fatigued worse from mowing than from any workouts as I struggled to keep course during the whole slow ride. My back ached.

Sweat burned in my eyes. Grass clippings stuck all over my sweaty body. Some clippings hit me directly in my eyes. So did bugs. That evening brought about relentless mosquitos, exacerbated by the stirring up and mowing of the lawn. They were the mosquito bites that hurt first before they itched uncontrollably. I pushed through. At the last moment before darkness, when my timeline and the gas in the lawnmower's tank had almost run out, I finished six hours of agonizing but necessary mowing in my back yard.

I smiled as I drove the mower into the overhead door on the side of my barn and through to the third room to park it. I stepped off the gas pedal and turned the key. The engine continued running for some reason, but I didn't care. I was going to let the gas run out on its own. As I walked from that room in my barn where I had parked the still-running mower, the engine exploded.

I slept well that Friday night despite the crystal. I had hardly slept that week. I had been stressed since reading that letter from the city. I put in arduous work fixing the mower, and I exhausted myself that Friday evening to complete my goal. I woke up refreshed. The line of crystal I sniffed from a glass chessboard added to my overall good mood. I could relax, and I could pick up where I left off. I sent Kelly a text.

"Third time's the charm. Life interfered twice, but I'm finally able to come see you. My next text will be when I'm pulling out of my driveway."

Two hours south of Perrysburg lies Wapakoneta, Ohio, the birthplace of Neil Armstrong. Wapakoneta is thirteen miles south of Lima and seventy-four miles north of Dayton...in the middle of nowhere.

At five o'clock that Saturday evening, I took the single Wapakoneta exit to buy some food and stretch my legs. The previous hour hadn't offered any fast food options besides Lima, a city I always tried to avoid. As I exited past the sign for the local space museum, I saw the golden arches to my right. I parked my car, entered the restaurant, ordered, and sat down to eat. As I got up to leave, I texted Kelly.

"I'll see you in about five hours."

I walked back outside and into the ninety-five-degree late afternoon heat. The sun was bright. There were no clouds in the sky. I sat down in my then extremely warm car and turned the key...nothing happened. I tried again. Still nothing. The starter was good, the battery was charged...the car was frozen. I pulled out my phone, and I video-called Kelly.

I watched as Kelly's eyes went from soft to angry. It was as if flames surrounded her face as we video talked. Kelly could not accept that it was the third time I wouldn't be able to keep plans to see her. The crystal had a hold of her independently from me.

"You planned this. You're a demon! You're a demon, sent to get my hopes up and crush them! You planned this from the beginning. You were never going to come see me!"

Wapakoneta was only one exit off the highway in the middle of farmland. I was in a fast-food parking lot in a sea of corn and soybean fields. There was one gas station within walking distance. There was a home improvement store within eyesight. I could see the last cars pulling from the parking lot. It was Saturday evening in the country. The store was closing for the night. Observing that scene brought a series of bad thoughts into my head.

Everywhere is closing for the evening. It's the weekend. I'm in the middle of nowhere. I sure don't see any auto repair places around. If there are any, they would be closed, not only in the evening but for the weekend. It's only Saturday. It's ninety-five degrees out. I don't have AAA. My car issue is beyond my skillset. It isn't even six o'clock. The sun is still going to be cooking for a few more hours. There's no breeze in the humid air. When the sun gets lower, the mosquitos will be out. It's about to be a rough night...

I couldn't do much under the hood due to the heat of the recently running engine and the brightness of the sun. I surmised though, that the issue was my ignition. Later on, two guys in their early twenties pulled up in a pickup truck and stopped to talk to me. One of the guys told me that he used to work at an auto shop. He did his thing and came to the same conclusion; it was the ignition.

The young men in the truck stopped by again later on in the night as I was doing my best to shoo away a strung-out vagrant before the vagrant figured out that I had something on me which he may have wanted. I explained to the transient that there was no way my car was going to move that night, so I wouldn't be able to give him a ride anywhere. The vagrant walked on. One of the guys in the pickup truck gave me the phone number of a mechanic he knew. He told me to call at eight o'clock the next morning. I thanked him. From there, I was physically alone for the rest of the night.

I made it through that miserable night in my broken car with company on my phone from two ladies from the website. One was in Pennsylvania, and the other was in New York. I got to know each of them. I was happy for the distraction from the bugs, the heat, and the boredom.

At one point, I walked to the close-by gas station. I bought drinks and snacks...and bug spray. I took as close to a bath as I could take in the bathroom sink. The second I walked back outside to my car, I was instantly again pouring sweat. I stripped to my boxers. It didn't help.

I called the phone number I had been given at eight the next morning. A man answered. His shop was on the other side of the small city, and his tow truck was on assignment out of town. I explained my situation and how I got the mechanic's number. The mechanic told me to sit tight for another half hour.

The mechanic pulled up in a short flatbed truck. It wasn't a tow truck though. It was just a flatbed truck. I texted both of my new lady friends goodbye, and I thanked them for staying awake with me. I then stepped from my front seat and met with the mechanic.

The mechanic had a flatbed truck with a tow hitch. He had cargo ratchet straps. He had an idea...the same idea which I had when I first saw the truck pull up. Twenty minutes later, I was skiing in my car behind the flatbed truck on the surface streets of Wapakoneta.

There was a good twenty feet of slack on the straps which tethered the front frame of my car to the trailer hitch on the back of the truck. The lack of power steering made for a challenging time at the wheel. The braking was a challenge as well.

After fifteen minutes of car skiing and concerned looks from other motorists on the road, I was pulled safely to the auto shop. Another ten minutes and fifty dollars later, and I was back in a fully operational vehicle. As suspected, it was an ignition issue. The security chip, out of nowhere, had stopped being recognized by the system. I was no longer headed to Kentucky. I drove to the expressway and headed back home.

Under a Dead Ohio Sky

I returned from another multi-week trip around the country as the summer of 2018 transitioned into autumn. I had one more lawnmowing to complete before the leaves fell and made way for a snow-covered Ohio winter. That night, however, my mind was elsewhere.

It was cold, dark, and lonely at my house that evening. Depression always hit me hardest when I began to feel the bleakness of a coming winter. The drugs helped, but the sadness always broke through. The solitude in my house that year was comforting and enjoyable…but it was also lonely. I knew, by that September, that I needed to make a change.

I had already decided to extend my travel plans from just the summer to an indefinite period. My next step was to end all the security and comfort to which I was accustomed. I loved my house. I had spent six years creating an environment exactly as I wanted within my walls. I knew that if I didn't let go of my home, I would never fully spread my wings.

The monthly house payment and bills were more than I could justify spending now that I was home only a week or two total out of each month. I felt the freedom of being jobless. I imagined more freedom without the couple thousand dollars of bills each month. I imagined how I would feel when I let go of the house I loved more than any other material item in my life.

I imagined warm locations in winter. I imagined a life of unfamiliarity and new opportunities. I had begun to get a handle on navigating the online world, the drug world, and the geographic world; all of which became my new life in 2018. I saw new possibilities on the horizon. I knew, just from all I had experienced, that there was so much more out there...

I thought about a lot of things that night. I did drugs as I interacted online. I had many shared dynamics. Sometimes someone would fall out of communication. Sometimes it took months. Other times, I would only be in contact with an online partner for a day or two.

I had long term dynamics, just a few, which began back when I first found the online world the previous winter. I had extremely close sexual dynamics lasting for weeks and months. Some dynamics were more loving and genuinely mutually caring. Some dynamics were specific and sex based. Some dynamics fell off fast for no reason at all. Ghosts and memories replaced interactions. Newfound dynamics replaced ghosts and memories. What filled me up inside also left me lonely and empty.

I livestreamed on the website that evening. I was taking a break from a downward spiral of thinking. My thoughts, like the sky that night, began to darken as the evening progressed. I caught myself slipping. I began the livestream, and I reset my brain while I appeased my online website audience. When I turned off the camera a bit later, the negative thoughts began to creep back in.

I began throwing out lines as the loneliness grew more pervasive. I checked some of my unread messages on the website from that evening. I copied and pasted a single message reply to anyone within a few hours' drive, anyone who had sent me a message of compliments or requests to meet me. I was calling anyone out on their messages. I sent my cookie cutter message to the first wave of ten or so people from the evening who messaged me. The message was basic and to the point.

"Hi. Pleasure to interact. If you are free tonight, I would be happy to see you. I don't mind the drive. Let me know."

Some messages went unanswered, or they weren't seen by the recipients. Some replies weren't what I was looking for. One reply from those first of my attempts to meet that night caught my attention right away. I looked at the sender's profile on the site.

The woman was nineteen years old. She lived in Columbus, Ohio. Columbus was two and a half hours from my house. The girl's message back to me was more to the point than my message to her. It was only one word. She simply told me, "Yes."

After my new Columbus friend texted back and forth with me for a few minutes, the girl asked me to make her a video showing my face and body. I told her I would as I got in the shower, and I asked her to reciprocate. I sent my video, I took my shower, and I watched the video she made for me once I had dried off.

My new friend sent me a video that was fifteen seconds long. She stood naked in front of a bathroom mirror. Her accent was strong. It was African. Her skin was a smooth deep brown. Her body was petite. Her black hair was shaved down short to her head. I dressed quickly and headed out.

I texted with my new friend as I drove down to Columbus. My loneliness had been cast aside. I was filled with anticipation. My friend had arrived from Uganda on an aerospace engineering scholarship two years prior. She was a junior at Ohio State. She booked a hotel room for the two of us that night. She sent me the hotel information. It was in Hilliard, just outside of Columbus. I typed the location into my GPS.

I stopped at a gas station when I was ten minutes from the hotel. I texted my location to my new friend. She texted me her room number. I was naïve and hopeful. I picked up some powdered donuts and milk for our breakfast the next morning. I got back in my car and hit another hotrail before I pulled out of the gas station.

"I just pulled into the parking lot."

"The door's unlocked. I just got out of the shower. I'm in the bathroom, drying off."

Leaving the cold and loneliness outside, I stepped into the hotel room. It was midnight. The drive from the Toledo area ate into the night. In a loud voice, I announced that I had food for breakfast in the morning. I got no reply. I spoke across the empty room to the bathroom.

"Hello?"

My friend walked out of the bathroom in a towel. I locked the bolt to the hotel door behind me. The girl smiled and dropped the towel. The two of us approached each other. We kissed as we stood in front of the bed. The girl began undressing me as we kissed. She bounced onto the bed to sprawl out naked in front of me.

After blowing down hotrails of meth all day, I was at a crossroads. My friend wanted me inside her at once. I knew the drugs necessitated foreplay to allow me to get hard. I thought of a solution. For the next twenty minutes, I made love to her between her legs with my lips and tongue.

I felt no loneliness after I satisfied my new friend. I told my friend I was going to the soda machine down the hotel hallway to get us some drinks. I dressed and stepped out of the room. I put money in the machine and walked back to the hotel room with two drinks in my hand.

When I walked back into the hotel room, my friend was still naked, lying on the bed, and catching her breath. I opened her soda for her and handed it to her. She took a big drink from the bottle and looked at me, incredulously. I smiled. My friend smiled back and shook her head as she managed to stand up from the bed.

My friend kissed me again as she walked by me to step into the bathroom. I took my clothes off, except my boxer shorts, and sat back on the bed…and that was when I felt the night's vibe shift to a weird space. A confused look crossed my face as my friend walked out of the bathroom, fully dressed.

"What's going on?"

"I need to go back down to the front desk. There was an issue with the payment."

I continued to look at her, confused.

"They called while you were out getting drinks."

I maintained the look of confusion. My friend hadn't

moved when I was out getting drinks. The phone was on the table away from the bed. The wet spot from my friend's orgasm was still under her butt and between her legs when I came back in with the drinks.

"Do you want me to go down with you to the desk?"

My friend insisted it wasn't necessary, and she was going to go clear up the issue on her own. She grabbed her bag and told me, in her thick accent, that she would be back soon. She walked out. I sat there on the bed next to the wet spot. Ten minutes went by. I texted to see if everything was all right. Five more minutes passed. My phone vibrated. I looked at the text from my new friend.

"I had to go. I'm on the way back to my house now. The room is paid for. Feel free to stay the whole night."

The cold and loneliness were then again with me in the room. It was just me, my empty feelings…and a wet spot.

Bad Mower Finger

My friend Tim lived in Findlay, Ohio in the fall of 2018. I'd met Tim through a series of interactions online. The two of us had been making videos and doing drugs when we hung out. Tim was an intravenous user of crystal. Even though I gave up the needles back in spring, I still shot crystal with certain friends of mine when I hooked them up with drugs. If I knew I was spending time with Tim, I fully expected to be poking holes in my arms.

Findlay, Ohio was forty-five minutes south of my house, on the route between Perrysburg and Columbus. I left the hotel room in Columbus the morning after I was ditched by the African girl from the website. I decided to spend the day at Tim's place before heading back to my house. I supplied Tim with the drugs he needed. Tim and I shot drugs and made videos for the rest of the day.

I left for home later that night. I knew I had been putting off that final lawn mowing of the year. I knew it was going to take a couple of days. The riding mower had been inactive ever since that day in late spring when it mowed its final time; that time the engine exploded as I narrowly avoided a large fine from the city.

I had borrowed a push mower from my friend Jane when I came back from Florida a few days prior. I was dreading pushing a mower, which wasn't even self-propelled, over an acre of what was once again far-overgrown grass.

I woke up the next day and blew down some hotrails. I checked the messages on my phone and began my daily ritual of interaction and video making. At one point, I went out front and began push-mowing my yard.

As I mowed, I continued replying to messages and interacting on my phone. One girl from the site was hellbent on coming to see me. I had work to do. The girl wanted to take a taxi the four hours from Cincinnati to my house. At first, I didn't think she was serious. By the time I finished mowing my front yard, I had to block the girl completely.

I went back inside midday to take a break from mowing. I decided to livestream on the website that afternoon. As usual, due to my meth consumption, I didn't reach climax. I was sweaty. I was overheated. I was frustrated.

Later that afternoon, I managed to break the compulsion. When I turned off the livestream camera, I got my hands free again to get some more actual work done. When I stepped out back to mow some more, I shook my head at the sight. I had managed the front yard. The grass in the back yard was longer, thicker, and it covered a much larger area...an almost endless sea of green. I knew I couldn't get it finished that day, but I had to try to get through as much as possible.

As the light disappeared that evening, I decided to leave the last quarter of the yard for the next morning. The grass the farthest back in the yard was the thickest and longest. It had given me trouble back when the riding mower was working. I was sure it would be no picnic with the small, unpropelled push mower.

I made it to the line in the yard where the far side of my barn lined up on the left. In the middle, at that line, was a lone flowering pear tree. Beyond that, the grass and weeds were a solid carpet of foliage stretching to the far tree line. The width of the area was at least three times the length. I planned to cut it in rows the next day, rectangles which would gradually become smaller as I finished. I figured I still had about three hours to go. Since I had thoughts to let go of my house, and northwest Ohio completely, I knew it was not just the last time I would have to mow that year. I knew I was about to be done mowing that yard forever.

I woke up the next morning with the goal of a mowed lawn in mind. I did drugs and got to work. Mowing that morning was different than the previous day. The grass was even longer. I went slower that morning. The grass was thicker. I only overlapped half as much with each pass of the mower. The grass was damp, the drizzle of rain from an overcast and cloudy sky mixed with the morning dew.

Every few steps, I had to push the handle of the mower down towards my feet to pop the deck and blades up into the air. If I didn't clear the blades, they would clog with the wet clumps of grass. Then the mower would shut off. I then had to bounce the mower up and down on the ground to clear out the obstruction before I could pull-start the mower again.

Clumps of wet grass piled up next to the rows as I mowed, in the rows I was about to mow. That added to the difficulty. The clumps I ran over again were enough to clog the mower and stop the blades. The grass in the rows was barely cut as the blades slowed and very often stopped completely.

Hours passed. My original timeframe, left behind like clumps of grass. Finally, I saw the end in sight; another five rows left. Another half hour at the most. I was getting impatient, and my mind was checking out. I began to take any shortcuts I could.

While holding the handles together to keep the engine running, I bent my knees and stretched my right arm towards the mower deck. I reached my hand into the chute opening, which led from the mower blades, to grab a clump of clogged grass. I heard the loud thud at the same time I felt it. My brain broke in reaction. In one motion, I yanked my arm back to my body as I stood up and released the mower handle with my other hand. The engine of the push mower cut off.

The air in the backyard around me became silent and still, a sharp contrast from the hours of loud lawn mowing. The last echo of the engine left the neighborhood and my brain. As suddenly as silence filled the air, the thoughts filled my mind. A million questions at once from all directions seemed to hit me in that first split second. Thoughts jumbled together and overlapped in my consciousness. I couldn't keep up. My rationale floated away with the last echoes of the then-silent lawnmower engine. I had no answers, but the questions piled in...

What was that terrible jolt I felt to the core of my body?
What was that sound?
What happened?
What do I do?
Do I still have fingers?
Do I still have a hand?

Stunned, I stood there next to a lawnmower in an almost fully mowed back yard. Time seemed to stop. It seemed like forever passed me by as I was hit with stupid questions and incomplete thoughts. My eyes, wide and unblinking. It was as if I was in a trance...

Should I finish mowing?
I'm almost finished.
Do I look down?
Yes...yes, I do.

I looked down. When I saw what the mower blades had done, I snapped out of my stunned trance. The daze I had been in, it instantly dissipated. Adrenaline filled me up. I then had a very real sense of urgency. I had transcended. A wave of panic washed over me. Three thoughts hit me at the same time.

I'm far out in my back yard.
I need to get to my house.
I'm hurt...badly.

I turned towards one of my back porches, and I ran. I felt the edges of blackness as my focus became tunnel vision. Adrenaline kept my feet moving under me while I felt the somniferous effects and impending unconsciousness of shock. I kept running. I reached the screen door handle. My left hand fumbled as I shakily opened the door.

I yanked the door open, and I stumbled across the patio. I looked down. I saw the trail of red behind me as I reached the door to my gym. I crossed the side of my gym and reached the door to my kitchen as the edges of my field of vision closed to black. I felt as if I was floating as I stepped through the doorway into my kitchen. There in my kitchen, the pain hit.

Though I never went fully unconscious, my legs took me no further than my kitchen. I managed to grab a dishrag from the handle of my stove before my weak and shaking legs succumbed to gravity. I was then on the floor. I writhed in agony as I wrapped the rag around my finger to stop the bleeding.

I managed to send a couple texts as I first sprawled out on the kitchen floor. I spent the next chunk of time in a semi-conscious and extremely painful heap on the Brazilian pecan floor of my kitchen. I lost concept of time, but I soon received a reply text from my friend Kate.

"I'll be at your house in an hour and a half."

Though Kate only lived fifteen minutes away in Bowling Green, she needed to drop her kids off at their dad's house.

The pain was unrelenting. It didn't come in waves, it was one constant tsunami...and I was crashing under it continuously. At one point, I managed to stumble my way through the house to my bedroom. I scrounged up a couple of weak painkillers, a beta blocker, and some benzos. I took a handful of pills. It was futile. Kate walked in to find me back on the floor of my kitchen, still in the same amount of pain. The rag on my finger was soaked in blood. There was blood all over the floor.

Hours passed that evening. Kate attended to me the best she could. I disliked hospitals. Kate was persistent with her attempts to take me to the emergency room. I knew I needed to go, I just didn't want to go. Finally, after twelve hours, the two of us agreed that Kate would take me to the emergency room after we had sex.

Despite the pain from the mower accident, Kate and I managed a half hour of foreplay. When the time came for the actual intercourse, pain and drugs basically eliminated any chance of being able to rise to the occasion. That was when I thought of an idea.

The prior six months, I had been involved in an online BDSM dynamic with a girl who lived a few hours away in southern Ohio. The dynamic was intense and intimate. The girl had even put me on a schedule of tasks and videos I needed to do for her. Some videos were a daily requirement. Some were to be made on a certain day each week. Some gave me creative freedom to think up ways to please her and build our dynamic together.

The day before, when I mowed my front yard and began mowing the back, I made a specific video to fill that creative requirement of the BDSM girl I was seeking to please. I created a video which ended up arousing the girl, and she gave me much positive feedback. First, I wrapped fifteen elastic hair ties around myself. I then spent the next couple minutes trying to pee with the hair ties squeezing me tightly. It was difficult, it came out in spurts, but I managed to make it happen.

I told Kate to hang on a second. There was an aspect of the previous day's video which was going to prove useful. It was a side effect I hadn't ever planned to implement. The pain in my finger persisted as I awkwardly wrapped myself with the hair ties.

In an act of carnal improvisation, with a bad mower finger, in pain, on drugs, and in a unique headspace, I consummated in a way I knew was a once in a lifetime event. Kate and I moved rhythmically together as my makeshift splint did its job.

It was the only time the two of us ever had intercourse. We had shared intimacy before, but never intercourse. In a weird way, I felt we had gone beyond sex that day. Kate then took me to the emergency room, after almost a full day without any professional medical treatment.

The x-rays came back. The doctor explained what was going on. The mower blade had completely broken the bone in my finger at the first knuckle. All bone was pulverized from that point to my fingertip. The hole in the end of my finger was where the skin had popped and expelled the pulverized bone fragments. The remaining bone slivers and shards were floating loosely in the end of my finger; internal splinters, sharp and jagged bone bits stabbing me from the inside. My finger had no solid structure from the knuckle on. It had begun to swell, and the pressure only added to the pain and discomfort.

That afternoon, three days into yet another lawnmower battle with my lawn, Kate finished the five remaining un-mowed rows in my backyard. It took her twenty minutes. I was done mowing the yard forever. After a summer of stress and problems and injuries, I was happy to be done. I didn't know it at that time, but I still had one last battle with my riding mower a few months later. For the time being, my focus was on my bad mower finger.

By the next day, my finger had swollen to twice the size. I made an interesting video trying to relieve the pressure as I drew blood repeatedly with a nineteen-gauge steroid syringe. Every few days, I had to remake the metal and foam finger splint to accommodate the inflation and swelling. Eventually, I had to use two splints as one to fit over the finger. I never followed up with the orthopedic surgeon to remove the bone splinters.

It Was Then

My life had gone off the rails. I was coming unglued. I held onto hope, and I had the idea to write out what was all mixed up in my head. I wondered if writing could possibly reel me back in. I knew my options. Maybe nothing would be better after putting my words to paper. I felt I was beyond reproach, yet I was still floating on the top of an iceberg, my head still above water. Maybe after all the time passed and all the words were expelled, I would find nothing was any better. Maybe I would still decide to take the long ride...

I was in the middle of a conversation with a girl in her mid-twenties from Ottumwa, Iowa. Our texting had begun a few hours prior, after she reached out to me on the website. It was after three o'clock in the morning on a Friday in the middle of October 2018. I had made subtle comments over the earlier few hours which hinted at my dark thoughts; cries for help. Even though I made sure to go under the radar, I still somehow felt better knowing I was sharing my desperation with another person.

The back and forth late that night with Iowa Girl deepened. She shared many thoughts similar to my own. Though Iowa Girl was talking of escape, my escape was something else entirely. Iowa Girl was in admiration of my recent dedication to travel. The escape I sought wasn't on a map.

"Where would you go if you could go anywhere?"

"I'd go back in time to find the version of me with my whole life ahead of me. I'd tell myself to pay attention."

"What do you want most out of life?"

"I want just one thing. I just want to be happy. With that, maybe I can feel I have a purpose. I could appreciate love. Maybe I could have it all. Maybe all else would fall into place."

"What will make you happy?"

"That's the part I can't get to. It's just out of reach…out of reach and in the dark. I told my mom I'd be okay. I don't know if it'll ever happen. If so, I imagine it'll just be for a fleeting moment."

"I wish I could help."

"Maybe you already are."

"Oh?"

Iowa Girl was starting to get tired as the night wore on. I had been tired for a long, long time. I said goodnight to my new friend. My focus shifted to the music playing in my living room on the surround-sound system. How fitting. It was the song I envisioned would be the crescendo as I stood at attention and put the handgun to my head to take that much-needed final sleep. The rest eternal; the rest for mind and body I needed after thirty-eight years of futility and waiting out an all too slow clock.

My eyes watered. I stood at attention in my living room. I was alone. I knew, when the time came, I would go out alone. I listened as the third and most powerful verse of the song, the song I chose to play me into eternity, began. It was fitting music to say farewell to a world where I didn't belong. It would float my spirit away as a bullet slumped my body to the floor for that final big sleep.

My last bit of sleep had been from eight in the morning to noon the previous day. Prior to that, I had slept until two o'clock that previous Tuesday afternoon. Two o'clock on Tuesday afternoon…the time I had plans to be somewhere else besides asleep on the couch in my living room. Two o'clock on Tuesday afternoon…

I was supposed to meet someone up on the north side of Detroit, Michigan. Instead, I woke up on my couch in Perrysburg,

Ohio. Had I run out the door and jumped in my car at the exact moment I awoke, I was still an hour and twenty-eight minutes away from where I needed to be. Two o'clock on Tuesday afternoon...

...

I had finalized plans that prior Sunday to meet a girl on Tuesday afternoon. Our first video interaction had me smitten. I was in full anticipation of our upcoming meeting two days later. Our first video interaction only lasted ten minutes, and the two of us both remained clothed as we made plans to meet and get to know each other.

I sat up quickly once I realized I had fallen asleep on my living room couch. It was two o'clock. It was two o'clock on Tuesday afternoon. I called Jay as fast as I could. She was understanding.

"I'm gonna shower now. I'll be there as soon as I can."

It was five o'clock when I finally pulled into the wrong end of the townhouse complex where I was to pick Jay up from her mom's house. I pulled in from the Eight Mile Detroit side of the neighborhood. The next street up was in Oak Park, Michigan. Jay's mom's place faced out to the Oak Park side. I couldn't drive to the other side of the parking lot from where I had pulled in. There was a curb and grassy median dividing the parking. I texted Jay from the Detroit side of the complex.

Moments later, I saw a small girl in a big winter coat walk around the side of the townhouses. Jay walked across the parking lot toward where I was parked. My heart began to beat faster. Jay continued the course in my direction. I smiled to myself as I unlocked the passenger-side car door. Jay got in the car and sat next to me. I smiled at her.

Jay was beautiful, with ebony skin, soft and flawless. She was 4'11" tall. Her petite frame, barely a hundred pounds, somehow supported her large pristine breasts and a perfectly round butt. Jay was nineteen years old, exactly half my age at the time. She was a dream which I was lucky enough to experience while awake. I lost myself in Jay's beautiful brown eyes as she gazed back at me. Her smile lit up my life. I was in awe of her and of being in her presence. Jay was an absolute ten. That afternoon, all my cares were left in Ohio.

I was living in the moment, wherever that moment was about to take me. Jay wanted Chinese food. She knew of a place close by to pick up. I called in the order. The two of us sat in the parked car for a moment and talked as we waited. A few minutes passed, and I drove around the corner to the restaurant on Eight Mile.

Another fifteen minutes of driving in Detroit traffic, and the two of us pulled into Hotel Royal Oak in Royal Oak, Michigan. I parked in the lot on the side of the building. I grabbed the bag of take-out food, and I walked with Jay to the door of the hotel lobby. I held the door for the goddess gracing me with her presence. I walked in behind her.

I checked in with the front desk attendant. I glanced over at Jay as she meandered between the chairs and love seats in the lobby of Hotel Royal Oak. When my glances met hers, Jay smiled at me from across the room. There was no way I was able to hold back a return smile. There seemed to be an electricity between us, like an unspoken vibe or an inside joke which was only there for us. Our subtle glances and exchanges made me feel alive. The fire was burning inside me, and I couldn't wait to be alone with Jay.

The anticipation continued to build as I signed papers and was handed keycards to our room. My heart seemed to skip a beat each time my eyes met Jay's. Jay and I held hands in the elevator as we headed up to our room. We were set to fulfill promises of our knowing glances.

As Jay and I finished eating, I walked over to maximize the air conditioning. Before I'd finished adjusting the wall unit to deliver the coldest possible air, Jay had removed her clothes. I looked back to the table and what remained of our meals. Jay's clothing was on the table next to the Chinese food boxes. Jay, in all her bare glory, was then close enough to touch…and I did.

We embraced before I even stood up from in front of the

air conditioner. My hands felt the soft skin of Jay's shoulders as she wrapped her arms around my waist. We kissed as I stood up. My mind exploded with fireworks.

Reminiscent of my very first kiss when I was fifteen years old, I was lost in that first moment with Jay. All my senses were alert and engaged. The moment belonged to the two of us and us alone. Time froze. The world stopped spinning. I became one with that beautiful creature. Jay was my everything in that moment. My world became her.

As we kissed, I removed my shirt...then my pants. I needed to feel as much of Jay's body as possible against my own. Jay and I wrapped up together as we made our way to the hotel bed. Magic was all consuming.

The year up to that evening, all of 2018, the entire year up to that point...the hookups before the website meetings, the exponential increase in sexual activity once I fully jumped into the online meeting aspects...the prior ten months of not just sex, but deep drug fueled multi-hour and even multi-day intimacy on unprecedented levels of creativity and depravity... all those on the spectrum, all types of people, across many states and in many geographic locations...in homes and cars, in hotels and outdoors...with all legal age partners from young to retirement age...all shapes, sizes, demographics...all personality types and demeanors...all levels of sexuality, sharing, and connection...with all experimentation and with all levels of experience...nothing but my own hand had actually physically allowed me to reach climax.

Sometimes, many times, even my own hand wouldn't get me there. There were times I would be close and fall short. There were times when others would get me close. I would fall short every time. Fortunately, my goal had always been to just live in the moment with another as we shared pleasure together. I was always more concerned with orgasms of whomever I shared intimacy with at the time.

That day in mid-October at a hotel in Royal Oak, Michigan, it only took fifteen minutes in the missionary position before I released inside of Jay. It was the first of two orgasms that night resulting from contact that wasn't my own hand. It was the first of two orgasms that night as a direct result of the touch of another person. It was the first of two orgasms from someone else in all of 2018. It began an eight-hour run of intimacy with Jay that night.

My first full length porn film was made from footage I recorded during that first night I spent with Jay. In my eyes, it was a work of art in and of itself. The movie was cut into an hour and one minute of our intimacy together. The only detractor, in my eyes, was the metal and foam splint which I was still wearing on my bad mower finger.

Jay needed to be back home after our sexual activity concluded. I didn't question why. We stopped off at a corner pharmacy. I bought Jay the emergency contraception pill, since I came inside her. I dropped Jay off back where I had picked her up. Once I saw she made it inside, I returned to the hotel room to finish out the night. A few days later, I gave Jay a burned copy of our movie.

The camera angles were as varied as the positions and activities which we engaged in during those eight hours of connection. The movie turned out wonderful because Jay and I were wonderful together. That first night we shared left me knowing I had found something special. I was enamored, but I couldn't shake a nagging feeling that something was off.

I First Felt It

Friday, three days later, I headed up to Detroit again to spend time with Jay. I hadn't slept at all after the conversation with Iowa Girl. That conversation lasted into early Friday morning. The thoughts of seeing Jay pushed my suicidal mentality to the back burner. We picked another restaurant from which to order food. We picked another hotel in a different part of the Detroit metro area to share a room for the day. We again shared magic together for many hours, making more videos together to document the experience.

Much later that night, Jay asked me to take her back to her house. That time though, she was staying at her dad's place. His house was in central Detroit, within the boundaries of the city proper. I dropped Jay off at her dad's house. That weird feeling which I experienced the first night was back in my head, but I pushed it aside.

Our days together continued with that pattern. We would order food from a new restaurant each time and find a new hotel in the Detroit area. Some nights, I attended to other business after I dropped Jay off. Some mornings, I picked her up again and we went to eat somewhere.

One night, after dropping Jay at her dad's house, I had almost made it back home. It was cold and snowing. The roads were slick as I drove on the highway through Toledo. On one of the overpasses, before the bridge over the Maumee River, a pickup truck suddenly spun out at sixty miles an hour a few hundred yards ahead.

The pickup took out two cars in the lanes to its left, on its way to slamming into the cement dividers on the left shoulder.

I managed to brake just in time to stop, only feet from impact with the driver's side of the pickup. I, being me, recorded a video.

The video suddenly became much more intense as I saw a tractor-trailer appear in all of my mirrors at once. I heard the constant blare of the truck's horn as the semi barreled towards the rear of my car. As I watched, holding my phone as it recorded, I was frozen. I had no time. Had there been time to react, there was a smashed pickup truck directly a few feet in front of me. The lanes to the right of the pickup had three other incapacitated and smashed up cars. Car parts were littered from one side of the highway to the other, and on the left side of my car was a cement barricade.

I remained frozen as the giant semi somehow managed to swerve at the last possible second. The doppler effect of the horn as the eighteen-wheeler careened by me, inches from smashing me to pieces, was deafening. As quickly as it all happened, I was suddenly out of immediate danger. I let out a breath I didn't realize I had been holding.

I sent Jay the video as I regained my composure. I told her in a following text how close I had been to death just then. About a half hour passed, and I was back home when I received Jay's reply.

"Glad you're ok. Talk to you soon."

I fell in love with Jay quickly, but I couldn't shake that nagging feeling that something was off. I stayed overnight in the Detroit area on nights when I planned to see her the next morning. She was always pleasant. Her mood was always positive. I learned from her to "be easy," as she would say.

I picked Jay up on a cold and snowy morning, and we went to eat and hang out at a coffee shop for a few hours. We cuddled by a fireplace and talked. She knew I felt something wasn't right. I had brought it up to her. For the first and only time, Jay's happy-go-lucky façade broke. Suddenly confused, I saw tears fall from her beautiful eyes. I pulled her close to me.

"What's wrong?"

"I hate what I'm doing to you." Jay's hitched words came through as she cried.

"I don't understand."

Jay cried for a few more minutes as I held her to my body.

"Don't cry. I want to protect you from anything bad. I wish I could take your sadness as my own."

I kissed her forehead. Jay gripped me back tightly in response. The moment passed. Soon it was as if Jay had never been sad at all. She was her beautiful, happy, bubbly self again. I remained confused for a moment longer. We left the coffee shop, and I dropped her off at her dad's house that afternoon. We both had other obligations that day.

I parked my car on the street a few houses down from my destination that afternoon. Colfax Street was in a rather uninviting area of southwest Detroit. I walked from a few houses down the street. I knocked on the front door. I was, according to my transgender prostitute friend, the only person she trusted to hang out in her living room. She let me in, and I sat down on a couch on the main floor. I knew she had company, both upstairs and down in her basement.

That day, I didn't sit long. My friend needed a ride down the street. She put on her coat, and I stood up again. We walked out the door and to my car.

I turned from Colfax Street. My friend directed me towards Gratiot. The two of us ended up on a side street, parked just shy of a cross street. Two car lengths ahead, parked perpendicular at the cross-street junction, was a police car... with an officer sitting inside.

The street where I parked was a one way. I was parked on the left. As the officer watched from his cruiser, or maybe he wasn't paying attention, a car with a chameleon paint job and completely blacked out windows pulled up on the passenger side of my car.

My friend's window went down. So did the driver's window of the chameleon car...but only enough for a hand to reach out. All I saw of whomever was in that car next to me was a hand, taking money from my friend's hand and reaching back out to give her a little bag. If the police officer had seen the transaction, which I couldn't imagine he hadn't, he didn't make a single effort to acknowledge either of our cars.

Soon, the two of us were back on Colfax. Once back inside the house, my friend cleared out the basement for me. I was tired. I wanted to rest, but I put a plan into action. My friend only liked snow, but her clients often requested ice cream. That was where I came in.

"Anytime you have a client looking to party, stop down here to see me. I'll make it happen."

It was an easy gig, at least so far during the daytime. I spent the rest of that week kicking back in the basement during the daytime while my friend rotated her clients through her home. Frequently, she would text me a specific number. I would put that much in a little bag. She would come down with a client's money and make the exchange.

The whole scene at that house was different when I arrived late-night one night after leaving my friend Kevin's apartment in Downriver. I had a backpack on me that night. In it, a metal pipe and a kilogram of meth which I had picked up earlier that afternoon.

A weird series of feelings washed over me as I was suddenly standing alone in that basement. Who was that second group of people who walked in the front door earlier and hurried upstairs? How many guys had come up from the basement before my friend directed me to go down there? How many people had I glimpsed for brief seconds during that hour while I was still sitting in the living room of that house, deep in the inner city of southwest Detroit that night?

The two point two pounds of crystal methamphetamine in my backpack seemed to weigh me down to the floor. The steel pipe next to the drugs on my back suddenly seemed too light, nothing more than a toy, a whiffle ball bat. A moment before I found myself standing there alone in that basement in Detroit, my friend had given me less of a request and more of a direction.

"I need to take a friend down the street to score a rock. Be right here when I get back."

I heard the front door close on the ground floor above me as people walked out. There was then just one pressing and pervasive thought in my mind, overruling all else.

Run.

Fortunately, when I ran up from the basement and out the back door in the middle of the night, I still had all of my belongings on me. I also still had my health. I ran through neighboring backyards to my car. I texted my friend as I sped away.

"Sorry, an emergency came up. I had to hit the road. Let me know later if you happen to need anything."

Calling Me Home

I picked Jay up from her dad's house in Detroit. I pulled around the block so we could sit and talk for a bit. She brought her new little dog with her that day. The dog was cute and well behaved. He sat in the back seats as Jay and I talked. Occasionally, Jay had to stop her dog from humping the back of the seat.

The sun was out that day, but every now and then a cloud passed overhead and dropped some snow. I thought I could finish the removal of the fingernail on my bad mower finger right there in my car. I recorded video of Jay being grossed out and laughing as I tried to remove the nail.

With the splint off, I pushed on the nail. It was only attached at the very top. I pushed the top stuck part down, and I showed Jay. It was gross. It hurt. I came close to finishing the job, but it just wasn't time yet.

When I went home that day, I convinced Jay to come with me. We first dropped off Jay's dog. She made sure I would bring her back home at the end of the night. Though I still found that to be weird, I was simply happy that she was coming back with me for the day. As soon as I got on the highway from the surface streets, Jay fell asleep. She slept until we exited the highway in Perrysburg an hour later.

I ordered pizza. Jay looked beautiful as she danced in her socks on the Brazilian pecan of my living room floor. The Sun's rays shined through the windows and reflected from the floor around her as she danced. She hadn't realized I was looking at her from the kitchen. Her bashful smile and look-away were super cute when she looked over to see me smiling in her direction.

I set up a camera with a full view of the section of my bedroom with my bed, and Jay and I made hours of video in my bedroom. I recorded just one time as we began making love. When I stopped the video at the end, it was four and a half hours long.

It seemed like so much time had passed. It was like the end of 2018 was a nonstop memorable experience. Jay and I continued making memories and videos together. I was in love. I felt I could give that girl all of me forever. I told her of my crystal use. She wasn't happy, but she didn't judge me. She wanted me to stop at some point. I told her I would stop by the new year. I meant it.

The weather was cold. The snow was lightly falling. It was barely noon one day as Jay and I were out driving in Detroit. I turned the music down in my car. As our seats stopped vibrating, I asked Jay what she wanted to do.

She was ready to get a room. I found one on the travel app on my phone. It was a motel that time, not a hotel. The two of us got the room key and drove around to the separate building where our room was located. We walked in the room as quickly as possible to get out of the cold.

That day, Jay and I made love for ten hours straight. Our clothes were strewn about. Our bodies touched every surface of the room. Jay was covered in my sweat. So was the bed. I was in heaven with Jay every time we were intimate. I was never happy when the time would come to drop her off. I couldn't get enough of her. I felt a way with her I had not felt in many years. I loved to see her smile.

The time came to drop Jay off at her mom's house that night. I didn't say much on the drive across the city. That nagging feeling was stronger than ever. Was it all in my head, or had I still been missing something? When I stopped my car across the street from Jay's mom's place, I turned to look at her. She looked back at me.

We held each other's gaze. Suddenly, Jay reached over and

hugged me close to her. We kissed as she released her embrace. Our eyes locked again. I felt desperation as her gaze was almost apologetic. Maybe she felt sad for me. Maybe it was something else. I sat, confused as Jay walked up to the townhouse complex where she lived. I sat there another minute once she was out of sight. I felt lost. I drove away.

I reached the motel about a half hour later. I had missed a turn due to road construction, and I had to backtrack. I was physically exhausted from sleep deprivation and ten hours of sexual activity. I was mentally exhausted. I felt my love slipping away, and I didn't know why.

I was eager to get back in the motel room, blow down some hotrails, and relax. I opened the motel door. As I walked in, my eye caught something I wasn't expecting. I turned to stare at the bed. My eyes widened. My heartbeat increased. I was in disbelief. It was something I had never seen, besides in pictures online.

I inhaled sharply and took a step closer to the bed. I held my breath as I leaned in a bit more. No way. There was no way. Jay and I had spent ten hours all over that room. Our clothes had been strewn everywhere. Our bodies had been together on all surfaces which could support us in any position. I leaned in just a bit more...

I watched as the engorged bedbug casually made its way from the top left corner of the bed to the bottom right corner. I froze for just a second. Then I grabbed two disposable translucent plastic cups from the bathroom. I caught the bug with one cup and quickly stacked the second cup into the first. I walked to the sink. I let a little water fill the space between the two stacked cups which held the bedbug.

I pulled my phone from my pocket. I got on an internet search as fast as I could. I searched for images of bedbugs. Yes, it was a bedbug. I was disgusted. I made sure I had all my items from the motel room. I left with the cups and walked to the motel office.

I walked inside the office as angry as I had been in a

long time. I thrust the cups out toward the desk clerk. I said some choice words, and I demanded my money back. I grew more angry when I found out the phone travel app was needed to reimburse me. I walked outside into the cold, and I left the bedbug cups for the motel front desk.

A half hour passed as I waited on hold with the travel app's customer service. I first had to deal with the refund. I then had to deal with no openings at any nearby hotels. I then had to deal with the fact the only open room nearby was a fifty-dollar upcharge from the room I had just vacated. I acquiesced hastily. I was cold and tired, still standing outside the motel office in the middle of the night.

I was mad. I felt defeated. The bug had grossed me out. I finally booked the only available room at a hotel. It was basically right across the street from the motel. I saw the hotel from where I was standing. I checked the reviews online. No sign of bedbugs in the patrons' descriptions of their stays.

I spread out all my clothes and items in the kitchen of the hotel room as soon as I walked inside. I did hotrails fully naked as I inspected everything. I shook out clothes. I emptied my pockets. I felt contaminated and dirty.

I texted Jay to have her call me right away. She read the messages but didn't respond. I was annoyed, and I left her a voicemail. I kept checking all my items the rest of the night. I checked the bed and the room as well. I decided to catch a few hours of sleep. From that evening, I began a new paranoia of hotel rooms.

The plan for the next morning had me picking Jay up from her house so we could go to an art supply store. She needed colored pencils for something. The two of us had decided to run that errand around ten o'clock in the morning. I hadn't slept for a while, so I ended up sleeping until eleven o'clock. I checked my phone when I woke. There were no missed calls or texts from Jay.

I called down to the front desk to secure a late checkout. I was good until one o'clock. I didn't text or call Jay that morning. I did meticulously go through all my clothing a few more times.

I seemed to be in the clear. I showered and did hotrails. Just before one o'clock, I checked through all my items one last time. I gathered all my belongings from the kitchen in the hotel room and walked out to my car.

I sat in my car for a few minutes. It was cold. I was cold. I looked at the screen of my phone. Nothing from Jay. I decided to leave Michigan. I wanted to go home and do laundry on an extra hot washing machine setting. It was gray and cloudy outside. The feeling I had inside me matched the weather.

I never saw Jay again after that day of the bedbug. She sent me a text the day after I came back home from Michigan. She asked if I was alright. I told her I didn't know. Two days later, I sent her a message; it was a farewell letter.

I told Jay that I loved her. I told her I was happy and thankful for all the time we shared together. I told her that whatever else was going on was okay, and I would always look back on our time together fondly. I told her I hoped one day she would find a love with openness and honesty, and with all she needs to be happy forever. I wished her the best always. I told her I would always be there if she ever needed me.

Jay replied to my letter. She thanked me for our time together, same as I had thanked her. She told me she would always have love in her heart for me. She told me she was sad it was the end. She said goodbye. I felt grateful for every moment I shared with her. I knew, even though I hurt, that any pain was completely worth it to be able to feel that magical feeling of being in love.

I was sad, but I let go of Jay that day. I reflected on my time with her. I reflected on myself, and on the things which I learned since my marriage had ended a few years prior. I thought about how my entire life had become something unfamiliar since 2018 began. I thought ahead to the coming changes in the near future. I resigned myself to my place in the universe.

I was set to move from my house in two weeks. I would no longer have the security of my residence. I thought deeply that day. I knew, beyond a doubt, that I was about to face life as I never had before. It was the end of November 2018. I had jumped into a new online world a full year prior. I had scaled up my activity in a drug fueled world as well. I left the corporate world in May, a world which I had served for two decades. I had all but dropped out of my familiar social circles. Lifelong friends still had a place in my life, but they were phased out to a minimum.

New friends and associations filled any gaps in my social world. New sexual partners, new online dynamics, and new business associates; friendships and genuine comradery were forged from like interests in substances and chance interactions online. I trusted some with my life. I trusted others only enough to know I wasn't in immediate danger. I cut ties anytime I felt something was wrong.

Token White

Makayla and I left her grandmother's house. Full stomachs from the holiday meal, we tossed our plates of leftovers in the back seat of my car. The two of us then headed to Makayla's mom's house. I took surface streets of Toledo that Thanksgiving to reach Makayla's mom's neighborhood.

In summer, the groups of teens in Makayla's mom's neighborhood would casually meander back and forth in the street. As my speed slowed to under five miles an hour, Makayla told me not to stop my car no matter what. I would creep through as the teens eyed me intensely. Seeing I wasn't stopping completely, the teens would eventually part in front of my car as I slowly rolled by.

The streets were empty that Thanksgiving. It was cold and snowing hard. The afternoon sky was gray and bleak. There were no leaves on the trees. Any ground not covered in snow was brown. It was the beginning of winter in northwest Ohio. There was nobody outside.

Makayla's mom's house was a crack and heroin den. I had come to my friend's rescue from her mom's place on occasions earlier in the year. People were sometimes passed out in random spots around the house. Furniture, floors…it didn't seem to matter. Wherever the drugs took hold was where the bodies lay.

I parked in the gravel in the front yard of the house. Makayla wanted to swing by and wish her mom a happy Thanksgiving. I figured I could trade someone some crystal and get some crack to mix in a syringe later on, back at my house. Makayla didn't use needles, but for some reason I really wanted to shoot an upper cocktail that day.

Makayla's mom Janet and some White guy were the only people in the house that day. The White guy was fifteen or so years older than I was, I guessed, based on his appearance. You never knew when it came to drug addicts, though. It was haphazard with age progression. I was thirty-eight. Most people guessed I was in my late twenties. I'd met people in their late twenties who looked well over thirty-eight. I shook hands with the White guy.

"Hi, I'm Doug."

"I'm Bob. Nice to meet ya."

I reached into one of my pockets. I tossed a bag with a single crystal to the table in front of Janet.

"Happy holidays, Janet. You know the quality level of my stuff. I'm looking to mix it up tonight. Toss me something back whenever you get around to it."

I then heard a noise coming from out front by my car...at least that's where I thought I heard it. I walked over to the front door. I told the people inside I'd be back in a minute. I walked out onto the front porch. I stepped into the frigid winter afternoon and closed the front door behind me. I then walked to my right, where I had parked my car in the front yard.

"I wasn't stealing anything, I promise!"

A woman quickly jumped up from the ground under my car. The lady's head popped up from the far side. I looked at her as she looked back at me over my car's roof.

"I didn't say you were."

The woman walked around to the passenger side of my car as I walked across the lawn towards her.

"I'm just trying to…"

She trailed off as a van screeched to a halt on the street in front of Janet's house. The side door slid open. Four large Black men were standing inside. One yelled to the lady.

"Come on!"

The lady looked at them. She looked back at me one more time. Instantly, she ran to the street and jumped in the van. The door slid shut. The van peeled out and disappeared around the corner. I was left standing there alone as the snow fell around me, confusion once more affecting the expression on my face. A few seconds later, I turned and walked back to the house.

Whiteboy Bob passed me the pipe. I hit the rock and sat down. After an hour, Makayla let me know she was ready to head out. So was I. Janet handed me a small folded up paper. I put it in my pocket. It was dark out. Snow had been falling heavily that earlier hour. It didn't look like it was going to stop anytime soon. It took a few minutes to brush off my car before Makayla and I left Janet's house.

The drive from inner city Toledo to my house in Perrysburg was treacherous. The snow reflected off the headlights in the dark. The snow decreased my already sub-par night vision. As we drove closer to my house, Makayla and I passed a couple of cars spun out in ditches. Fifteen minutes stretched to a half hour. Once home, I was happy to be in for the night, out of the cold and dark…

Makayla and I took our coats and clothes off in the living room. I pulled the folded paper from my pocket before taking off my pants. I retrieved a spoon from the kitchen drawer. I set it on the table by my laptop in the living room before I went down a hallway to the bathroom to find a cotton swab.

I came back and slid a syringe next to the spoon and cotton on the table. I took a crystal from a bag and shaved off a few points onto a digital scale. Then, I used a blade to push the pile onto the spoon. I squirted a few points of water onto the powder and dropped a piece of cotton into the suspension. I then unfolded the paper Janet had given me.

"Aw, man…"

I didn't get crack to mix with my crystal…I got heroin. I thought on it for a minute. What could I do? I was in for the night. I had drugs. It looked like I was about to do a heroin and crystal speedball instead of a crack and crystal cocktail. Whatever.

I dumped the entire contents of the paper onto the spoon

and mixed it up. I sucked the contents up from the spoon through the cotton and stood up next to the table in my living room. It was time for me to get lit.

The act of injecting high purity crystal methamphetamine was a unique and multifaceted experience. Once I found a vein, I would pull up on the plunger just a slight bit to see that the blood registered in the barrel. Then I would push the plunger until the syringe emptied. That was where the ride began.

Ice would flow up my arm, a second later the taste would hit the back of my throat. One more second, and the heat would hit the palms of my hands, the soles of my feet, the base of my skull, and my b-hole.

A split second later, I'd involuntarily inhale sharply as the rocket fuel took hold. That breath would begin the hyperventilating. There would be times I would jump up to my feet and run out of the room.

Moments later my breathing leveled out. I would be left with what I called googly vision. The surface heat wore off quicker than the googly vision. Ten minutes later, I would recover from the superficial effects. My brain would remain flying high for hours.

Injecting meth was, by far, the most instantly overpowering method of administration. After the spring of 2018, I had very much varied my ROA. I mainly stuck with sniffing lines until my friend Kevin introduced me to the hotrail method. Hotrails became my preferred method from there. Injection kept a spot in rotation, depending on who I was with or my mood on a particular day.

Every ROA of crystal was a distinct experience. I found insufflation, despite the first brain burn, was a pleasant and comforting high. Eating crystal would require the least re-up maintenance. The physical effects of eating crystal, such as feeling my heart pounding in my chest, tended to be too much. Smoking was a fast wave of pleasure, washing over me and moving on quickly. Smoking required more continual use. Plugging, or "booty bumping," needed a precision for which I usually didn't have the patience.

When Kevin introduced me to hotrails, they instantly became the route of administration I used ninety percent of the time. The positives of that method were numerous: the buzz of both sniffing and smoking, no burn if done correctly, easy, enjoyable to conduct, not much prep time, and the pipes became reserves to scrape instead of opening a bag and breaking up another crystal.

Heroin, in contrast, was completely different. I had sniffed it and smoked it many times over the many years. Up until I was in my early thirties though, shooting heroin was by far the method I would use most often. The rush from heroin is nothing like the rush of crystal meth, base cocaine, or cocaine. The intravenous prep method was the same with heroin as with other injectable hard drugs. Once it was pushed into a vein, that was where the experience diverted.

Heroin took a few seconds to hit. I would first feel it in my lungs and chest. It was as if my breath had been taken away from me for just a second. Then, a microsecond later, waves of pleasure, and comfort, and contentedness would flow over my brain and wash out through my body.

Heroin was somniferous. To what level was dependent on potency and quantity used. It was a walk on a razor's edge, such as was cocaine when injected, but it was the exact opposite side of the blade.

That Thanksgiving in 2018 was about to be the first time I had injected heroin in years. It was about to be the first time I had injected heroin since well before I was using crystal daily. I was careless. I hadn't factored in the compounding effects of drugs on my system. Though I had the amount and potency of my crystal down to a science, I was not factoring the potency or quantity of heroin I was about to compound.

I stood in the main living room area of my house. Makayla

was lying on a couch across the room. I pushed the mixture into my circulatory system. A second later, it all hit at once. I became nauseated and dizzy. I stumbled to the couch. I put my head in Makayla's lap. The cold and black of that snowy Ohio evening permeated me entirely.

I didn't know how much time had passed, but I woke up momentarily to water thrown in my face. I stood up, I mumbled something short of words, and I stumbled to the kitchen sink to fill up a cup of water. I managed to chug the water as my knees gave out on me. I realized I was on my way to the floor. The darkness moved again from my periphery to consume me.

Again, time passed. Again, I woke up to water in my face. Makayla helped me back to the couch. My head lay in Makayla's lap. She stroked my head as I went to sleep. Something in that hazy moment let me know I was through the worst of it. I slept peacefully as my friend watched over me.

I was lost in the first moments of reanimation as the sunlight shone bright in my living room. I was at home. I was in my house, and it was daytime. I felt rested.

Makayla walked over to me from the kitchen area. She looked down at me as I rolled over to face her. I was naked on my couch. Makayla was wearing underwear.

"I wasn't sure you were going to make it. I was close to calling 911 and taking off before they got here."

"Thanks for the vigilance last night. Somehow, I always make it."

"You need to watch out. I was worried."

"Yeah, no more of that for a while. I should have specified to your mom what I wanted to trade. Oh well, it's over now. What do you wanna do? We should get some food. I'm not really feeling Thanksgiving leftovers right now."

Don't Get in Your Own Way

In the six years I lived in my house, my marriage, my family, and my hopes of someday bending to fit into that world not mine, it all fell by the wayside. Any love I felt was fleeting, whether it was for others or for myself. My love for my house was stationary. It was my sanctuary from the pain of outside misalignments. It was a comfort when the familiar became too much to shoulder. It was my love when I could not find any love for myself. My home was a distraction from my own head when I was inside both.

I questioned if what I was doing was what I should be doing. It was different, it was uncomfortable, it was uncertain... it was exactly what I needed to be doing. I stayed the course. I sucked it up and emptied my house over the course of the following week. Whether it was through sales, storage, or moving into the room I began renting at my friend Jane's house...I painstakingly emptied my belongings from a place no longer my own.

Memories of a past squandered were intermingled with specters of poignant recollections. My life, as was dust in the wind, blew away in the air. Who I was, as was sand on a beach, washed away into oblivion. Again, I questioned if what I was doing was the right choice for me.

I had zero ambivalence when it came to one item of mine. I knew I was very ready to sell that item. I even accepted a mere fifty dollars for it. It was my old nemesis. It was my riding mower. The mower managed one more parting shot that year as I helped the old man lift it up into the bed of his raised pickup truck. As I went to push the mower into the truck bed, the old man's grip slipped just a little. I had to push quickly to keep the mower from dropping down to the cement garage floor, and I tweaked my back.

December 2018; the six years in the house I loved had ended. I had sold my favorite car from my garage. I had sold off furniture and items to downsize. I had the items I wished to save, stored in a fifty-two-foot trailer at a building which my stepdad owned. The items I wished to keep close went with me to my friend Jane's house on the outskirts of Perrysburg. My travel items remained in my car.

At that point, I knew my future was going to be dedicated to travel. I wanted to keep a local mailing address. I wished to keep a homebase, a place to sleep when needed, a place to regroup and recharge. I offered Jane a monthly amount, and she was happy to rent me a room. I loaded the room with a refrigerator, a microwave, an entertainment center, and all kinds of other items spared from the storage trailer. I even decorated my space with a few small fountains I bought on impulse while tweaking on crystal during various trips to local stores.

My room at Jane's house was just as comforting to me as the house I had moved from, just on a smaller scale. On the one or two nights I spent there each week, I filled my time with tweaked interactions online. I created media, I exchanged sexts, and I interacted with intimate online partners on live video.

I was out of town at least five nights a week. My friend Kevin's apartment in Downriver, just south of Detroit, was an easy jump-off point for my many destinations around Michigan. Kevin, his girlfriend Sasha, and I hung out and did hotrails during the days. Kevin's friends from the Monroe and Detroit area were in and out all the time. I always let Kevin handle transactions. Kevin took the notoriety he seemed to relish amongst his friends. I maintained a position to remain disconnected and anonymous.

There was a girl on the eastern side of Ohio whom I had been sharing online time with for a while. I freed up one evening. I agreed to see the girl out near Cleveland where she was living.

I always dreaded that boring drive between Toledo and Cleveland on the Ohio Turnpike. It was a straight shot east from my house. It was only a couple of hours, but I never looked forward to taking 80/90 either direction. That evening, the drive wasn't as unpleasant as it usually was. I had anticipation as fuel for my trip. The crystal and the anticipation were a pleasant mix.

Dawn and I both felt our meeting had potential to be magical. We were both excited. We had shared fantasies as we became familiar with one another over the previous weeks in contact. She was adventurous, for sure. She was twenty-nine years old and hadn't had much connection which she could utilize to indulge her fantasies. I was ready to be that blank canvas for her to paint with her desires.

Dawn met me outside as I pulled up to her house. She showed me where to park. It was a large farmhouse which was split into upper and lower living spaces. She lived in the upper section. We climbed the stairs to the second floor. She held my hand and guided me through the threshold at the top of the stairs. We went inside the house.

Once inside, I set my bag down and stripped off my winter coat. Dawn brought me a plate of chicken and potatoes which she cooked for me. We sat on her couch together as I ate. We talked, sharing prolonged eye contact…the connection amplified. I knew it would. It always did.

Dawn and I shared thoughts and fantasies. We shared hopes and ideas for the future. We shared past personal moments. We opened up to each other as I figured we would. We smiled as we talked. I ate the food Dawn had cooked. I drank a large glass of juice to wash it all down. I reached over to touch Dawn's hand, and I rubbed her hand with mine.

"No matter what you desire tonight, I want to show you

how beautiful intimacy can be. I want your fantasies to become our shared memories."

Dawn had done hard drugs on random occasions. She had never done crystal.

"I want to try it."

"I have a wonderful way for you to first experience it."

"I trust you."

I took the needed items from my bag and set them up.

"Be ready when I kiss you."

Dawn nodded her head. I did a hotrail as she looked on. I reached a hand up behind her head and palmed her hair. I pulled her mouth to mine. As we kissed passionately, my mouth transferred the smoke from my lungs to hers. We disengaged, and Dawn licked my lips. I whispered to her.

"Exhale."

Our eyes never broke gaze as smoke from Dawn's mouth filled the air around our heads. As she finished breathing out, we instinctively kissed again. While Dawn and I undressed each other, we did all we could to keep our lips and tongues intertwined. It was as if we were polar-opposite magnets. The attraction was impossible to deny. Our drug fueled night was underway.

"I've never opened up to anyone like this before."

"The drugs have something to do with that."

"I already planned to give you my everything tonight. I've been thinking about you since we first connected."

"Well, I'm happy to hear that...but the drugs are still part of it."

Dawn was creative. She had fantasies for which she sought an outlet. She was as ready as I to push limits and experiment together. She was willing to be fully open and vulnerable. Dawn wished to share everything with me... everything except one thing.

An oversight was impossible in that instance. It was an omission which only could have been deliberate. Dawn knew she kept a huge secret from me as our night began. The shock of the reveal the next morning didn't just catch me off guard. Dawn had lost track of time by then. The timing surprised her almost as much as it had me. Neither of us knew what was coming, though. All of our thoughts were in the present moments we shared together.

"Intimacy can include anything. The deeper our shared connection and the more open we are, the more we become one."

"I've never met anyone like you. You've really opened my eyes. I can't believe there's this entire world I haven't seen until now."

I looked deeply into Dawn's eyes.

"I'm yours...yours to show you the world you have yet to see. I'll obey any wish you have. The more unique it is, the more we become one as the moment becomes ours. Anything you've kept to yourself because you didn't have someone who's sole fantasy was to see your fantasies come true..."

Hours passed. Neither of us noticed. We were so lost in each other. Dawn let her lust override her self-preservation. I was still completely in the dark. She was too, but only because our intimacy was consuming all her thoughts. She should have been up front with me before I even showed up. She could have been up front with me at any point over the entire night. She never said a word. I was set to be blind-sided in a terrible way.

Hours later, when intimacy had peaked, we were both content. We had done much together. We both had made memories only we would ever share. It was seven o'clock the following morning. The two of us dressed. Little did I know, new memories were about to be burned into my brain. Those memories involved someone else entirely...someone whom I was never given notice even existed.

As I sat in the living room, fully dressed and packed up to leave, the door to the upper section of the house opened and slammed shut. A juiced up and wild-eyed man ran in and instantly began yelling. First, he yelled at Dawn.

"What is this, Dawn!? Who is this guy!?"

My eyes widened to match the new guy's eyes. I was

shocked to see the fiancé Dawn said was no longer in her life standing irate in front of me in HIS living room. I grabbed my bag and began to step to the door.

"What are you doing in my house!? This is my house! That's my fiancé! You shouldn't be here!"

"You're right man. I'm leaving. No worries..."

I kept repeating in a calm voice those three sentences. The guy was right in my face. He followed behind me to the door by the stairs.

"You don't know how close you were to dying today!"

"You're right man. I'm out right now..."

I made it to the landing at the very top of the stairs. I had a hand in my pocket. My other hand gripped the railing as I put a foot down onto the top step. Dawn's fiancé was directly behind me. He yelled nonstop. I stayed calm as I half-expected a kick to my back to send me to the bottom of the steep staircase.

The kick never came. I descended the stairs at a normal pace. Dawn's fiancé stayed at the top. He stared daggers as I walked out. He yelled again.

"You're lucky you didn't die today!"

I reached my left hand into my left pocket to pull out my car keys. The hand which I kept in my right pocket since I had been at the top of the stairs inconspicuously put the safety back on my handgun. Had I been kicked down the stairs, I would have shot that angry guy. I was never touched. I started my car and drove away.

I was meeting up with people from the online world most days each week. Sometimes, I met with multiple people in multiple cities on the same day. I was all over the place. I had time, I had the desire to meet new people all the time, and I loved to drive all over the place. Everywhere I went, I also had trusted associates to interact with in other ways to fund my constant travel. Sometimes the online world and the drug world would overlap and fill all my sexual and financial needs in a single stop.

A week after I left Dawn's fiancé's house, I was sitting on my bed at Jane's house scrolling through my phone. I noticed a message from the website. I opened it. It was a first-contact message from someone in Florida. Zoe told me she appreciated what I had written in my profile. Her message wasn't the generic comments on my pictures and videos. She had taken the time to read and digest what I had put out there in the sections of my profile which gave insight into who I was. No played-out compliments or superficial observations, Zoe just shared understanding and commiseration. She had my attention.

Zoe quickly gave me her phone number after a few back-and-forth messages on the website. We switched to texting. It was only a matter of minutes, and we were talking on the phone. That night, Zoe invited me to Cleveland two weeks later. Another boring dreadful drive across the top of Ohio... I seemed to be making that trip frequently as 2018 came to a close.

Zoe lived across the country where the palm trees and sunny beaches stayed warm in the winter months. I was confused as to why she was coming to Cleveland, Ohio in the first place, especially in the depths of a cold Midwest winter. Zoe invited me to stay the whole weekend in her hotel room.

Zoe never blatantly said it, but she was a person of note in the LGBTQ community. I only figured that out when I searched her name online after our first phone call. She was national level mainstream. She had been for years. She never played up that angle with me. A pageant with Zoe's namesake was taking place over a weekend in Cleveland. It was to become an annual event. She had to be there to oversee it and host it. She wanted me there for the non-pageant aspects of the weekend.

I found a parking space at the hotel. It was a busy area of Cleveland, just east of downtown. I had to drive through the maze of traffic-congested interconnected strip mall parking lots to park on a slant at the hotel. I was up against a hill of plowed snow from earlier that evening. It was the only place to park.

Again, I told myself that I was not going to be in the Midwest for any future winters.

I checked the room number Zoe sent me when I arrived. Zoe had flown into town early that morning. She had spent the day overseeing the first setup and first show of her event. She had been back at the hotel for about an hour when I arrived. I stepped into the hotel elevator and hit the button.

I knocked twice on the door to Zoe's room. I had butterflies in my stomach. Zoe opened the door seconds later. We smiled and locked eyes. Zoe's tan skin was a contrast to her white bath robe. The cleavage between her breasts, a golden bronze. I assumed it was intentional, how her robe was undone. Zoe's eyes still managed to capture my gaze more than anything else…just barely, though.

Zoe had me undressed by the time I was through the door. Her lips and mine danced together. I disrobed her. When the two of us reached the bed, we were both fully naked. We fit together perfectly. The magic was instant…the intimacy unparalleled. We both felt transcendence that evening. The night was ours. Nothing else but our pleasure permeated our thoughts.

Hours passed. Zoe and I had melted into each other. We were soaked in each other's sweat. We pulled into one another's bodies. Our lips interlocked. We reached climax together.

The two of us took our first break from each other's bodies to do some crystal. We both had crystal. My crystal was a bit better. It was always better. I used to try other varieties when other people randomly had their own. One hundred percent of the time, I would then tell them to put theirs away. The rest of the night was always on me.

I wasn't just being hospitable in those instances. From day one, way back in spring 2017, I was a crystal snob. It not only worked out for me, but for anybody who happened to be around. It never failed to help build my trusted clientele. It never failed to spare me from an inferior product going into my body. It never failed to treat whomever I was with to an unlimited amount of a substance beyond any potency they had known before. A true win-win…win, win, win.

    Zoe and I each managed two hours of sleep early that next morning. I woke up to Zoe's alarm. We were still cuddling, and Zoe opened her eyes right after I did. There was light coming through the sides of the window curtains. I knew Zoe had an extremely busy day. I knew we both had to get up from bed.

    I put on my clothes and grabbed my bag. Zoe and I kissed a bit more. Zoe stepped into the shower as I stepped into the hallway of the hotel. The door shut behind me, and I walked down the hall towards the elevator. I had another stop to make while I was in the area that day.

Record Lows

A deep cold hit the Midwest during the 2018/2019 winter. The last weeks of January 2019 were poised to set records and pose a very real health risk for residents of the fly-over states. Wind chills below negative forty degrees Fahrenheit swept in, and the cold settled deep.

Cars failed to start, and ice on the frozen roads was so entrenched that no salt or plows could remove it. I had spun out before in rain, snow, sleet, and ice, conquering horrible weather and driving treacherous roads, but I had never seen anything like that winter. Driving even at five miles an hour was too fast, making it impossible to control a car on ice that cold.

I had always loved extreme weather. I was twelve when I saw my first tornado and had chased them ever since. However, that winter's weather was not the type I wished to chase. It physically hurt in seconds, and one breath in that frigid air took the life from my lungs.

Worry was on everyone's mind at Jane's house. We feared the pilot light on Jane's furnace would go out, or the furnace would fail against the workload, leaving us without a heat source. Despite the insulation, just a few days into the super-chill, the temperatures stole the heat from the house. Space heaters couldn't keep up, and it took effort to resolve the situation. We managed the problem, with the help of Jane's ex, who was an electrician. It was a legit, life-or-death, time-sensitive situation, and teamwork proved essential between the three of us. Finally, we had heat in the house again, but the cold outside was sticking around for the long haul.

In the week before the deep freeze set in, I first interacted with a girl from the website who lived in Tiffin, Ohio, an hour southeast of Toledo. That following week, fully immersed in the devastating cold, I headed to Tiffin. Tiffin was a small city surrounded by farmlands. It had a legitimate small downtown, but barns and tractors lined the highways in all directions from the city. Flat fields encompassed the countryside, barren and snow-covered through the winters; stereotypical Midwest.

I parked on a downtown street and took a short, fifty-foot walk to the Tiffin apartment. The wind burned my face and fingers, and I could barely open my eyes. There were two flights of outdoor stairs exposed to the elements leading up to the apartment door. After a minute and a half outside, I cursed all of existence as I shivered down to my bones.

Hailey let me inside. Her apartment, though not as cold as the wind-whipped outside, was still below freezing. Her utilities had been shut off, and it was her last day in the apartment as she had been evicted. Hailey, a Toledo native, grabbed her bag as I prepped and blew down a couple of hotrails. The drugs did nothing to warm up my core.

It had only been five minutes since I first stepped out of my car. The heat in my car had quit working back in late fall, making the cold even worse. I had been driving around that winter with nothing but my own body heat for warmth. I managed fine until the really cold weather hit, a battle I couldn't win.

When I picked up Hailey that day, I knew I was in for some chicanery. No matter how cold and uncomfortable I was, I knew Hailey had to be feeling worse. That day, Hailey had begun her second day of heroin withdrawal.

I had a rule for myself the whole time I lived with my friend Jane. I never brought or invited anyone to Jane's house. Jane allowed me to live with her and her two adolescent sons, but my business, whether work or pleasure, was always handled elsewhere. I never had friends over.

Besides the mutual friends from my home city I shared with Jane and the friends she herself invited over, everyone else remained in the dark about my residence. It was drug-induced paranoia, but also my diligence to protect my friend and her kids.

That first night with Hailey was a long one. I drove her from Tiffin to inner-city Toledo. We stopped on a street near my grandma's house, a neighborhood I knew well from years prior. I remembered waiting on those streets for heroin dealers, the stress through the roof as friends ran inside houses to score drugs. The longer we sat in cars on those streets, the more likely we were to be approached by police...or worse.

Hailey claimed we had stopped at her aunt's house to pick up some money. I didn't say anything but thought otherwise. Sitting in my cold car on that cold street, I had that same feeling from all those years ago.

I didn't feel the need to call Hailey out on her maneuvering that evening. As the sun went down, it grew colder. Hailey insisted she needed only eighty more dollars to get her apartment back. After a few fruitless stops, I finally reached my limit of patience. Just before dawn, I stopped by an inner-city carryout, withdrew eighty dollars from an ATM, and gave it to Hailey. She promised to pay me back, but I knew I would never see that money again. I didn't care. I was cold and needed heat.

I picked a hotel from my travel app and began driving towards West Toledo. It was after six in the morning, and I had to try for the earliest of early check-ins. Both Hailey and I shared the same physical symptoms from the cold, our legs burning and numb simultaneously. I thought we might be in the first stages of freezing to death.

As we drove by a house that jogged my memory, Hailey heard me laugh to myself. She inquired, and I told her a story from the house we had just passed, one that had taken place only months before.

I had met a lady on the website...the same site where I met Hailey. I drove out to her house. She wasn't the lady from her profile. If she was, then her profile pictures were at least a decade old. I decided to walk in and sit down anyhow. I kept rejecting the lady's advances. She kept walking upstairs for a minute at a time.

I was about to get up and leave. All of a sudden, an older angry guy in his white brief underwear stomped down the stairs. The guy had a seventies blacksploitation moustache and an attitude. He yelled just a couple sentences at me before stomping back upstairs.

"Hey man! My sister tells me you're a nice guy, but you need to pay her forty dollars! What don't you understand about giving her the money!?"

I didn't even bother to unholster my gun while at that house. I kept it secure on my ankle. After the brother went back upstairs, I got up to leave. The sister tried to get me to stay. I threw two twenties on the floor in front of the couch. I had been hoodwinked. I paid forty dollars for that life lesson.

Hailey laughed a little. She told me that what happened to me was unfortunate. I remained silent. I was thinking how Hailey had taken me for twice that amount of money just an hour before I told her that story.

Freezing in my car, Hailey and I made it to a hotel on Reynolds Road in Toledo. It had been a battle, the entire night, to see through the windshield of my car while driving. Our breath in the frigid air had created a situation where ice formed almost instantly on the inside of the glass. I constantly used an ice scraper on my windshield as I drove. I pulled into what I guessed was a parking space in front of the hotel. I greeted the Indian man at the counter.

"No rooms this early."

"We've been in my car all night without heat. We can't last much longer…"

The man took pity on me.

"Give it half hour. Come back then."

Hailey and I walked together to the shower in the hotel room. We spent the rest of that day in our warm room, fully naked and making videos. The cold outside raged on. Our minds were elsewhere for the time.

It reached six thirty the following morning. Hailey and I had spent a full twenty-four hours of warmth in that hotel, but I had to be somewhere. I showered again. I hurried and dressed.

"Where am I taking you?"

It took me fifteen minutes to scrape the ice from the inside of my windshield. All the ice shavings fell onto my dashboard. My car was running the entire time, and it didn't heat up inside at all. I ran back upstairs to tell Hailey the car was ready to go. I hurt everywhere from the cold. I tried to focus my thoughts away from the fact that Hell had frozen over. The drugs were no match for the Ohio winter.

I didn't expect any relief from the cold for the next hour. I had a drive ahead of me to the Detroit airport. It was seven in the morning, and I was on the interstate heading north, out of Ohio. The sun was shining that morning. No clouds were in the sky. It was bright to the point of distraction as I crossed into Michigan.

I was so cold, and the light reflecting from the ice all around me was making the drive one of the most dangerous trips I had ever taken. Cars around me on the highway were littered about on the sides of the lanes. Some cars had obviously spun out on the ice. Others sat more orderly and straight. They seemed to have given into the cold, abandoned by their drivers. I knew that if I succumbed to either of those fates, if I ended up on the side of the road, I would be in for a terrible death at the hands of the Midwest winter temperatures.

After a white-knuckle drive, I finally pulled into the Big Blue Deck parking garage to store my car at the Detroit airport. I began to ascend the levels of parking. I was pushing it for time, but if I could park and get through security inside the terminal in the next hour, I would be able to walk to the gate just as boarding was about to begin.

I kept climbing the parking levels, driving in circles to make my way higher. Panic began to fill my mind. Panic eclipsed my hatred for the cold when I reached the top level of the parking garage. An hour had passed, I had scoured the entire complex…there was nowhere to park.

Defeated, I wound my way back down through the parking garage. My flight was scheduled for departure in fifteen minutes. I called the airline as I heard other flights above me taking off and landing. Twenty minutes of explaining, being put on hold, and explaining again secured me a different flight… along with spending four hundred extra dollars…and along with a twelve hour wait until my new departure time.

I had twelve more hours in the frozen wasteland of the Midwest. I left the airport to take another hour-long drive back the other direction, another hour without heat. The cold once again became my focus. Hell…it really had frozen over.

I ran from my car into Walmart when I reached Perrysburg that morning. The heated store felt amazing. I sat on a bench inside the store for ten minutes before I was able to walk into my bank. I decided the thousand dollars in cash I had in my pocket was better off in my bank account. I deposited the money, leaving me with four dollars in my wallet.

I was so hungry. I went to the grocery section and picked out a few things to eat. When I went to pay at the register, my debit card was declined. I protested, then I walked back over to my bank. I explained the situation to the bank teller. After another fifteen minutes with the bank teller on the phone, I was told my money issue had been resolved.

I went back to the checkout line and tried to pay again. Again, my card was declined. Again, I walked over to my bank. That time, after a few more minutes, I was told I would be able to use my card in another fifteen minutes. I walked back outside without waiting around. I was ten minutes from Jane's house. I would eat when I got home. The cold outside the doors of Walmart abruptly ended my hunger. I had no choice but to switch my focus from eating to the very real possibility of freezing to death.

I thought, by midday that day, I would have already left the Midwest and the nightmare cold. I was supposed to be on my approach to my destination as I sat in my room at Jane's house and thought about the day thus far. I snapped out of my daze, and I informed Madison of my new arrival time to Kalispell, Montana.

I thought ahead to the evening. I got online and searched parking lots close to the Detroit airport with shuttle service to the terminal. I found an independently run parking lot four miles from the terminal. I pulled my debit card from my wallet to book a reservation for a parking space ahead of time. I wasn't about to head to Detroit again without a secured parking space.

When my card was declined, I called my bank's customer service department. Unlike the bank teller, physically standing before me at my bank earlier, the lady on the phone explained to me what was going on. Since it wasn't me who directly rebooked my flight earlier that morning, my debit card had been flagged.

When I gave the lady at my airline my card number, she bought me the new ticket from her office in Houston, Texas. That out-of-area transaction signaled fraud to my bank. That action put a block on any further transactions. It was the reason I wasn't able to buy food at Walmart that morning. It was why I couldn't book a parking reservation with that debit card.

The issue with my bank flagging fraud from the rebooking of my flight was resolved after some stress and more time on the phone. I then kept my card out, and I reserved a parking place at the offsite lot in Detroit. I planned to head out from Jane's house early enough to give me time to park, take the shuttle, and board my flight with ease.

The cold had permeated my car's engine when I went to leave Jane's house. My luck was proving to be bad all day long. Somehow, I eventually managed to start my car. I wasn't worried about time. I had plenty. The cold was again my immediate concern.

Fifteen miles up into Michigan, I decided to stop in Monroe for some fast food. I still had plenty of time. I was halfway to the airport. I was hungry. I exited the freeway, and I stopped at a drive-thru restaurant.

I ordered my food and pulled around to the restaurant window. I opened my car door because my window was frozen shut. I opened my wallet to get my card to pay. I had eaten only once that day, right when I reached Jane's house in the morning. I was looking forward to the fish sandwich, chicken nuggets, and fries. It was worth feeling the frigid air slam into me as I opened my door at the pick-up window.

The cashier extended her hand from the drive-thru window. My response was unexpected. I opened my wallet, and a two-word sentence escaped my lips.

"Oh, no!"

I still had the four dollars in my wallet. I no longer had the thousand dollars in my other pocket. That cash was in my bank as of that morning. The issue with my debit card had been resolved. It was fully useable with no issues...except my card wasn't in my wallet. It was on the table in my room at Jane's house, left there after I reserved the parking space.

Hunger, and even the cold, were once again pushed from my mind. I suddenly had bigger issues. I had a choice to make. I was still good on time, but that would all go out the frozen window if I opted to try to make it back to recover my debit card. I pulled away from the drive-thru with nothing to eat. I made a choice.

I was going to head to the northwest corner of Montana with only the four dollars I had in my pocket. I wasn't going to miss a second flight out of that terrible Midwest winter Hell. I was going to travel across the entire country without enough money to buy a sandwich along the way. I got back on the freeway, and I drove north from Monroe, Michigan.

I found the parking lot up by the airport. I was hungry, cold, and fed up with the day's ridiculousness. I parked in the congested snow-covered lot. I did the best I could to shield myself from the wind, and I slid my way across the lot to the shuttle loading area. Before I could reach the small metal overhang, the shuttle left for the airport. I spent another fifteen minutes of standing in high winds and negative temperatures.

"When You Hear the Sound of a Kitty..."

  I spent the first flight to Salt Lake City hungry, but at least I was warm. I knew I needed good luck when the plane landed at the next airport. I hoped the arrival gate was close to my next boarding gate. The departure time of my next flight out of Utah was only fifteen minutes after touchdown of the flight I was on.

  I stood anxious as I waited to get off the plane. The minutes ticked away as I couldn't progress my situation until I stepped off the airplane. I finally stepped into the terminal, and I checked the map to see where my connecting flight was boarding. I had fifteen minutes…and my flight was on the opposite side of the airport. I ran. I dodged people and anything else in my way. I made it to the gate as the doors were closing. An airline employee held the door when she saw me approaching. I walked quickly down the ramp and into the aircraft. I reached my seat and sat down. I was out of breath and pouring sweat.

  I walked from the ramp and into the Kalispell airport. The vibe of the building was rustic. I first saw Madison through the glass of the doors as I walked to the front of the outdated airport terminal. We smiled at each other. Madison and I then did as we had discussed prior. The two of us pretended to act out a scene like in a movie. We ran in slow motion towards each other and embraced. We kissed like the actors who pretended to have been apart for so long. I told Madison I had always wanted to do that. It was a bucket list ridiculous item. It was then a new memory.

I threw my bag in Madison's SUV. We both got in. We made eye contact, and Madison pulled off into the Montana night. Something about that look in Madison's eyes before she began to drive us to her house…

As Madison and I traversed the night, she pointed out places and buildings in her city which held significance in her life: the post office where she worked after she left the military, the bar where she sang karaoke, the streets and businesses which shaped and influenced her life during the twenty-six years she lived there…the school she attended as a child, the details of her life in Montana.

That night, Madison came to bed with me in a spare bedroom at her house. We kissed and felt each other for over an hour. Madison and I reached a point just short of intercourse. Madison eventually excused herself to go sleep in her bedroom. She told me to get some rest. She had plans for our first upcoming day together.

We were up early that next morning. We went and ate breakfast at a diner in town. Madison then took me to Glacier and took me to Whitefish. I loved everything we saw. The mountains, the sky, the water…the whole experience seemed surreal. It was the last day of January 2019. I left a Midwest winter which was so cold it was dangerous. It was forty degrees in Montana that day. The two of us wore hooded sweatshirts as Madison took me to some of the most beautiful scenic locations I had ever visited.

It took three stops that day for me to find a Western Union to receive five hundred dollars. I then had money again. I felt it would be enough to get through until my online money card cleared and was active. Though I didn't have my debit card with me, I had received a card from my other account days prior to the trip. It was only coincidence that I had done the requirements to start its activation just two days prior.

Madison took me to a grocery store that evening. Her mom was coming to eat dinner with us. We picked up the items to cook, and we headed through the beautiful Montana landscape, back to Madison's house. After Madison's mother left that night, we shared a repeat of the night before. Again, Madison retired to her room just short of intercourse. I didn't mind at all. It was never about sexual consummation. Anytime I hooked up with anyone, it was always about the connection we shared.

That intimacy between Madison and me concluded the first full day of the two weeks I was to spend in Montana. News from the East was of no end to the bitter cold. It felt like spring to me in Montana. I slept well that night, knowing I had more ahead to experience. Before I drifted off to sleep, my mind flashed back to that moment my eyes caught Madison's eyes as we pulled away from the airport. Something about the look in her eyes in that moment...

Madison's passion was singing. She had a favorite location for karaoke. It was a large, square building on the outskirts of Kalispell. The two of us passed it on the way to Madison's house early in the day.

"Do you wanna go there later? You can meet some of my friends. I'll sing for you."

"Sure, I'm good with whatever."

The big sky was dark when we pulled into the bar's parking lot. We walked inside, and I was surprised by the number of people inside a bar in Montana in the middle of the week. For some reason, I wasn't surprised at the taxidermized polar bear behind glass along an interior wall of the building.

I could see that I was in Madison's world. Madison lit up as soon as she was inside the building. She knew everyone. Two tables of her closest friends sat around talking about what songs they were going to sing that night. Madison made her way to all the sections of seating to say hello to people. People came up to her and requested songs for her to sing. She introduced me to people all around the bar. I smiled, seeing she was in her element.

The deejay announced Madison's arrival on the microphone when he saw her. I sat with her and her friends. They drank. I didn't. Madison sang a few times as she rotated turns with her friends. I watched her performances and clapped for her. Then, suddenly...I was alone.

As the night went on, I stayed in the main seating area by the stage. Groups of people sat or congregated in haphazard locations throughout the establishment. A couple of hours passed by without me seeing Madison. I looked for her. I asked her friends. They told me that she was with other friends in another spot in the bar.

I checked to see if Madison's car was still there. It was. I ran into Madison and two of her friends as I walked back inside. She apologized and told me she was in a conversation of importance. She said it would not be much longer. I went to the restroom in the bar. I then went to sit in Madison's car in the parking lot. I wasn't mad or annoyed. I was just more comfortable in the seat of a car than a chair in a bar by myself.

Madison jumped in her car about twenty minutes later. She began apologizing profusely. She then asked me a question I didn't see coming.

"If we stopped by and got your bags, can I drop you off at the airport?"

"What? My flight isn't for almost two weeks..."

Madison and I talked as we sat in the car in the bar parking lot. There was a guy Madison had known her whole life. Between the time Madison and I first interacted on the website and when she picked me up from the airport, she and the guy had become something of an item. She told me they had always had crushes on each other, and they both had learned that information about each other just recently.

"I'm so sorry. I didn't plan for this."

"I get it, but it puts me in a predicament...I saw a look in your eye as we pulled away from the airport. Was that it?"

"Yes. I've been talking it out with him all night tonight. It's why I disappeared."

Madison and I spent the next day together. She took me to her favorite restaurant for lunch. We watched a couple of movies. She gave me her bed to sleep in that night. She took the guest room.

The next morning, I checked my online cash card. It was active. I booked a hotel for the rest of my time in Montana. Madison took me to an ice cream shop. She then took me to a grocery store so I could shop for food for the hotel stay. When we reached the hotel, she put the security deposit on her credit card. My cash card wasn't accepted for that part of my stay.

I had a week and a half to spend in that hotel in Kalispell, Montana. I didn't have a vehicle, I didn't know the area, and all my friends and connections were elsewhere. I hadn't done any drugs those days I was at Madison's house. Those days were the longest I had gone without drugs since I first began using crystal in early 2017, almost two years earlier.

I wasn't at Madison's house anymore. I was on my own. I was on my own...and I did happen to have a quarter ounce of crystal with me. It was a quarter ounce I had brought with me through airport security, in my pocket. It went through the conveyor belt x-rays and all checkpoints. I figured out a way to carry it with me and not get caught.

Once I was alone in my new hotel room, I set up and prepared to get high. I had been so consistently on crystal that I was sure I still had plenty in my system. Despite not having a clean slate, I knew I was still going to get extra zooted after taking that short break. I sniffed my first line. It was half a gram. The burn subsided and I was flying high in that hotel room.

At one point, I accidentally dumped two grams of powder on the hotel carpet. I rubbed it in with my foot. I wasn't about to do hotel floor drugs. I still had five more grams. I would make do with what wasn't rubbed into the floor.

I was on overdrive with my online interactions. I knew I was trapped at that hotel, but I embraced physical isolation. I had three visitors during my hotel stay. I had many new online partners keeping me company at that hotel. I had even met a lady from Atlanta who shared the first draft of her memoir with me for my critique and edit.

Though it was winter in Montana, the weather was mild. I found a Mexican restaurant within walking distance in the snow. Mexican food had always been my favorite. I ate at that restaurant two or three times a day. I also found a thrift store in the general area. On a few afternoons, I visited the store.

My last morning in the hotel began stressfully. I woke to news alerts all over my phone. There was a terrible winter storm working its way across most of the country. My flight was in the late evening. The storm was building momentum by the hour.

Minneapolis was to be my layover that day. I was originally scheduled to fly into the Minneapolis airport and then fly on to Detroit. Minneapolis was one of the first major airports which shut down that day due to the storm. That began a long back and forth phone battle with my airline. As I figured, I wasn't the only person that day trying to sort out my flight schedule.

As soon as I thought I was set with a new return route, as soon as I felt relief, the next airport would shut down. I would hop on the phone again to start the process all over. I would receive email updates every few minutes from the airline. I could hardly keep up.

Your flight has been cancelled.

Your new flight will be at this time going to Atlanta.

Your flight has been cancelled.

Your new flight will be at this time going to Chicago.

Your flight has been cancelled.

Your new flight will be at this time going to Dulles.

Your flight has been cancelled.

It just kept going. Hotel management let me stay throughout the day as I tried to get together some semblance of concrete flight plans. By dinner time, I convinced the airline to concede to an idea I formulated.

The airline rescheduled my flight for the half dozenth time. That flight had a connection in Tampa, Florida. From there, there was no connecting flight. The Detroit airport had shut down as well.

After much talk and negotiation, after being transferred to other customer service reps and their supervisors…I was set up with a plan which made me happy. It was time to leave the hotel.

I left the hotel with a ride service that evening. The car dropped me off in front of the Kalispell airport. The snow was falling hard. The sun was almost gone. I then had a couple of hours to wait and hope my outbound flight didn't get grounded. I had finally taken some solace in my current situation.

I was headed to Tampa. I was on my way to see Bryan. The airline worker told me that I could catch the second leg of my flight three days later. I would be able to spend those days warm in Florida. I would be able to spend the time with a best friend I had known since I was fourteen.

Bryan was the first person I had done drugs with, almost a quarter century prior. We took some paper acid during our first year in high school. We split our time that night between an outdoor party in the woods on an island in the Maumee River and a house party at a friend's house a mile away, in the Fort Meigs neighborhood in Perrysburg. We were high school freshman. We had just opened the doors to a new world of drugs. Our journey had begun.

Five years later, I lived with Bryan in Fairborn, Ohio. For a year, as Bryan went to college, I grew weed in our apartment in the Dayton suburbs. It was the one time in my life I didn't live in the immediate Toledo area. Bryan and I were well-versed in almost all of the drug scenes at that point.

Bryan and his brother had moved south in the early 2000s. Each year, I always went to visit. Charlotte, North Carolina was where they lived for years. They then moved to Florida. I continued to make trips. Girlfriends came with me. I always loved my time with both brothers. They were two of my closest friends.

It had been a year since Bryan found his brother dead in their shared home. I knew Florida had been hard for Bryan since then. I had gone to see him multiple times in 2018. Each time, I had been closer to convincing him to come back up to Ohio. This time, I hoped to succeed.

When I arrived on the plane in Tampa, I took in the warm weather. I texted Bryan to let him know I was at the airport. He didn't reply. I spent the next couple hours wandering around the airport and eating food at restaurants.

Finally, my phone call woke Bryan up. He told me to meet him. I flagged down a taxi and told the driver my destination. I was going to a storage yard in Clearwater. Bryan told me he would be waiting for me there.

Oh, How Things Can Change

It was a hot and humid evening in early 2019 in Clearwater, Florida. Bryan and I walked through the boat and RV storage yard. As the two of us walked between campers and speedboats, I told Bryan the surprise I experienced upon walking away from corporate America the previous year.

That fear of not having the security of a job quickly gave way to a new feeling of freedom in late spring of 2018. That freedom was compounded in November of that same year when I also walked away from my house. I stepped from the ledge, and 2018 had been the year where I left the world I knew in northwest Ohio. I told Bryan I had no idea what I was doing, but I had taken a step towards hopefully finding myself.

Bryan unlocked and opened the door to his fifth wheel RV. I followed him and stepped inside. Things were different that time. The large camper no longer looked like a living space. Boxes and items were stacked inside, filling the space almost completely. It was hot. The air was stale and unwelcoming.

When my friend Makayla took an impromptu trip to Florida with me in the summer of 2018, that camper had been Bryan's home. It sat on a lot in a camping community in Clearwater Beach. The air conditioning blew chilly air into the comfortable and homey living space. There was running water and electricity. Just thirty-seconds of a walk away, there was a clubhouse with laundry facilities. Just beyond the campground walls, there was a beautiful beach and the blue waters of the Gulf of Mexico.

I thought back fondly to that trip just months prior. It

seemed a world away. Each night, I dropped Makayla off at a hotel somewhere in Tampa. I secured a room for her before heading back to Bryan's RV, where I would spend each evening with my friend. While Bryan and I did drugs and hung out, Makayla used a website to make her money as an escort. I took solo trips for random meetups with ladies from the internet, ladies who reached out when they saw I was in the Tampa area. Most of my time was spent catching up and reminiscing with my old friend.

Sometimes I took quick trips to Makayla's hotel to drop off party favors. Other times, if she had a ride, Makayla swung by Bryan's RV so I could supply her with what was needed.

Each morning, Makayla found a ride back to the RV or I drove to pick her up and bring her back. She then gave me the money for the previous night's hotel room. During the next day, Makayla decided if she was going to stay longer at the same hotel or find another place for the upcoming night.

In that summer of 2018, Bryan was big into injecting speedballs of heroin mixed with crack. I stuck mainly to crystal. The two of us were both down in it, but I was still not fully off the rails. I expressed my concern with Bryan's addiction from a hypocritical position. I made sure he knew I cared about him. I knew it was up to him to change…if he was going to change.

Bryan and I shared a long history of heroin together, one which began in high school. We knew the pain of the drug. We knew the pain of losing people we loved to heroin. I had, for the most part, left that drug in my past while in Ohio. Bryan and his brother had stayed the course those years when they were down South. I hoped my concern for my friend had been a positive force on Bryan as we each injected our drugs of choice together in his RV in Florida.

That visit in early 2019 had a different feel than the visit with Makayla six months earlier. There was an urgency to it which I felt in each moment. Bryan's fifth wheel was now just a storage box. His health had declined, and his mental state had also slipped. He was homeless since his camper was in storage. Bryan and I had gone in under the gate and walked through the storage yard just to have a secure spot to do drugs. It was far too hot and humid to stay longer than ten minutes in Bryan's camper without electricity or air conditioning. I asked my friend what had happened since the last time I came to see him.

Between the trip I took with Makayla and that current trip, I had come to see Bryan another time. It was in fall of 2018. That trip was a positive trip as well. At the time Bryan's RV was put in storage, he secured a posh spot on a golf course in Sarasota. A woman he knew through his father allowed him to stay with her in her house on the golf course, knowing he had no options at the time. Bryan had food, shelter, and security for a brief time in the fall of 2018. I stayed with him at that house for a week. He had a good situation going. Shortly after I had gone on my way, all that fell apart. Bryan told me he had been caught up in the heroin scene again, and his dad's friend became wise to his activities. He was promptly asked to leave. He had been homeless ever since.

I was concerned for my friend during the three-day unplanned visit in early 2019. I felt Bryan's desperation. I felt his defeat. I did all I could to convince him to leave Florida as we walked the back streets of Clearwater. Those weren't the streets or places shown on the vacation brochures.

Bryan and I waited at a donut shop one evening to go on a drug run with some people he knew from the scene. We went to a hotel and waited in the car while others went inside to score. We managed to stay that night at a house Bryan's friend owned in the Clearwater area. That next day and night were spent in a drug fueled haze at that house. I began interacting with a woman from the website while I indulged in a menagerie of hard drugs along with Bryan and four of his friends. The woman from the website was eager to meet.

On the day before I was to fly back to Detroit, Bryan and

I were dropped off at a fast-food restaurant. The house party was over, as the work week began for those friends Bryan knew. Bryan and I ate food and then hit the streets to walk. Florida was perpetually hot and humid. I spent that day talking with my friend. I finally heard what I hoped I would hear.

"Alright…give me time to wrap things up. I'll come up to Ohio soon. I need to start over."

"Happy to hear it. I'm worried about ya, man. I look forward to seeing you up there."

Bryan was alone in Florida. He had been alone since a night shortly after I joined the website a year prior. He had been alone since a night back when my friend Angie and I began making videos for the website. He had been alone in Florida since I got a text that night a year prior, and I took a break from creating sex-based videos as a more pressing issue developed.

"Dude, my brother died."

Bryan had been alone in Florida since the night I stayed on the phone with him, at a loss for words as paramedics wheeled his brother's body out while I listened. Bryan's brother had been another of my best friends. Alex was two grades below us in school. He graduated with my sister. Both Bryan and Alex were as much my family as they were my friends. Alex's death was only a year after their mom passed from cancer. Bryan was family to me, and he was all that was left of his own family. I felt good as I parted ways with Bryan that evening before my flight back to Detroit. He was coming home.

Rita, the lady from the website, pulled into the parking lot shortly after the sun went down. Bryan and I hugged. I again told him I looked forward to seeing him up North soon. I walked over to the silver Benz and got in. The car drove off.

Rita and I shared a nice evening after she picked me up. I spent an hour lying on a couch at a tattoo parlor. Rita had an appointment to finish a tattoo, so I lay there and thought about Bryan. I also thought about the time I spent in Montana which led to me being able to spend those days with Bryan. Once the tattooing was finished, Rita and I walked out to her car.

A half hour later, the two of us arrived at Rita's townhouse. It was a classy home. Rita was classy. She cooked me the absolute best street tacos I had ever eaten. She did my laundry. She set me up in a big comfortable bed. I got good sleep before I had to be up four short hours later.

That next morning, Rita made me breakfast. While it was still dark outside, she drove me thirty minutes to the airport in Tampa so I could catch my early morning flight to Detroit. The two of us hugged, and I thanked her for the much-appreciated hospitality.

Wasn't Life Almost Worth Living?

Prior to leaving for Montana, the freezing weather had been unbearable. After I returned from Florida, the extreme cold had ended. It was still winter in the Midwest, but the weather had faded into a backdrop for my activities. I could function in my day-to-day life without the immediate threat of freezing to death.

After my friend Kevin and I blew down a bunch of hotrails, I gathered up my belongings from Kevin's living room. The two of us walked out of the apartment to my car. The bass from the music in the car was deafening, so our drive wasn't filled with much discussion. After fifteen minutes on the roads, I pulled into the parking lot outside Kevin's workplace and dropped him off for his twelve-hour shift on an auto parts assembly line.

"Get a hold of me once you're off work. I have a stop to make right now, but then I'm gonna head back to Perrysburg and catch up on sleep."

I was still in the parking lot at the Detroit auto factory when a text came through. I heard my phone vibrate, but I finished hooking up the wires to one of my new speakers before I checked my messages. Ten minutes passed, and I finished the wiring. I hopped back in the driver's seat of my car. I picked up my phone. The text was from my friend Bryan. It was only one sentence. I smiled as I read it.

"I'm here."

I pulled out of the Detroit parking lot and called Bryan as I drove to the interstate. He didn't answer. Once I crossed from Michigan to Ohio, my phone began to ring.

"Where are you?"

"I just got off the bus. I'm at Cherry Street Mission downtown."

"Alright, man. I'll text you when I get there."

Fifteen minutes later, I pulled into a small parking lot across the street from the homeless shelter in downtown Toledo. I sat in the parking lot and did drugs as I waited for Bryan to come across the street from the shelter. After ten minutes, he came out. He had two bags with him. I stepped out of my car and opened up the back door so he could throw his bags inside. Bryan and I hopped into the car. I drove through downtown Toledo, back to the highway.

I decided I was going to get a hotel room. I drove with my friend to Reynold's Road. Just off the 80/90 turnpike, there was a hotel I frequented with ladies I met online. I knew the price was reasonable. More importantly, I knew the hotel was free of bedbugs. I made a reservation as I drove to our destination.

That first night in the hotel, I spent time catching up with my friend of a quarter century. We talked and got high. We did hotrail after hotrail. We left to get food. Once back to the room, the two of us continued doing drugs and talking. I covered the room's smoke detector with a plastic grocery bag. I wanted to be sure the smoke from the crystal didn't set off the smoke alarm. At one point, Bryan fell asleep. He was exhausted from the three-day bus trip across the country. I retired to the bathroom to interact with others on video. Eventually, I too succumbed to sleep.

After I woke up that next morning, I paid for another night in the hotel room. I retrieved breakfast from a fast-food restaurant for the two of us.

"I gotta leave for a bit. I have to stop up at my friend Kevin's."

"That's fine. I got back in touch with some of the high school crew. Aaron's coming to pick me up."

"Hand me that torch. Let's blow down a couple more hotrails quick. I'll hit ya up on my way back from Detroit later on. I shouldn't have too many stops to make."

I had been texting with a girl from one of the dating apps. On my way back down from Kevin's house, I texted Bryan to let him know I was going to stop to pick the girl up. He texted back, he had met a girl who had a hotel room across the street from us. He planned to stay at the other hotel that night.

That next morning, I took my lady friend back to her place. A half hour after I arrived back at the hotel, Bryan knocked on the door. I was in my boxer shorts doing hotrails. I unlocked the door and let him in. He hit the pipe and went ahead to tell me his plans going forward. I was happy to hear he had worked something out.

Bryan told me how he spent time together with our friend Aaron from high school when I had gone up to Michigan the day before. Our friend Aaron was, at that point, the manager of an inner-city apartment complex on the edge of downtown Toledo. Aaron offered Bryan an apartment in his complex. He also gave him a maintenance job at the complex.

"How soon is all that happening?"

"Both the apartment and the job are good tomorrow."

"That's great. I'll get this room for one more night. Let me call 'em quick."

Two days later, my phone rang. I answered as I drove down the highway.

"Hey man, you able to swing by and run me to the store? I need some groceries."

"Yeah, I'll be over."

"I'll also get money out for you."

"Don't worry about giving me money. I'll be there soon."

Bryan opened the door and welcomed me into his new apartment. Though his home was in a rather unpleasant area of Toledo, the living space was nice. He had a corner unit on the ground floor of a six-story building. Two sides of the apartment had large windows. The windows illuminated the living space with rays from the sun. He had a full kitchen to the left, beyond the living room. Across from the dining area, there was a hallway to his bathroom. A little farther down was Bryan's bedroom. It was a basic layout, and all the rooms were spacious.

I drove Bryan to the Walmart in Perrysburg for some grocery shopping. The two of us hit some hotrails in the parking lot, and we went inside the store. After Bryan found the items he wanted, we stood at the register of a self-checkout lane. Bryan paid with a card, and he selected cash back. He handed me a twenty-dollar bill. I looked at him, confused.

"I told you, I don't want any money."

"It's for the crystal…and gas money for driving me here."

I had two thousand dollars hair-tied in a folded stack in my pocket. I reluctantly took the bill from Bryan and added it to my stack. I turned from the checkout lane where he was ringing up his items, and I began walking towards my bank at the front of the store.

"I'll meet ya by the exit doors after I drop this money in the bank."

As I took a couple steps towards the bank, I heard something that would haunt me. I almost missed it. It was only one sentence. Bryan had said it to himself, not to me. I was facing away from him when I heard it. I was already a few steps towards my bank. Had I been in thought of almost anything else at that moment, those words Bryan spoke would have slipped away into the air. I heard him though, as he spoke under his breath to himself.

"Doug and I are squared away."

I froze mid-step. I turned back to look at him. Bryan wasn't looking in my direction. He had been gathering up the bags of groceries from the register. I stared at my friend for another moment. As if I saw a ghost, I was frozen in my tracks. He kept gathering up his grocery items. I slowly turned back towards the bank. I pulled my focus away from my friend, and I resumed my walk.

On the drive back to Toledo, I was deep in thought. That

moment at Walmart had burned into my brain. I couldn't shake it. I helped Bryan bring the grocery items into his apartment. He didn't ask for any more crystal when I was on my way out. I didn't give him any. He had to work the next morning.

"I'm happy you're back, man. I think it'll be good for ya."

"Yeah, I think so, too. I'll see ya soon."

I was on my way back up to Detroit. I had work to do that night. I drove towards the highway. That sentence I overheard Bryan say to himself echoed in my head that entire drive to Michigan. I couldn't get that moment from my mind. It was so out of character...whether he was saying it to me or just to himself...

The next couple of days, I mostly spent at Kevin's apartment, but I also bounced around between a few other spots in the Detroit area. I drove back from Michigan to Jane's house in Perrysburg late Friday afternoon.

Bryan and I often spoke on the phone back in high school. Once text messaging became a thing, we both texted each other frequently. He texted me at four fifteen on that Friday afternoon as I drove back to Ohio from my friend Steve's place. It was a straightforward text. I read it, but I didn't reply.

"Finally off work. Time to relax for the weekend."

I didn't hear from Bryan that weekend while I was back in my room at Jane's house. It seemed odd, but I didn't think much of it. He had the weekend off work. I figured he had been taking it easy after his first week of work. He wasn't yet adapted to a work schedule. It wasn't until Monday when Aaron, our high school friend, sent me a message. At that point, I put some things together in my mind.

"Have you heard from Bryan? He didn't show up to work today, and I can't reach him."

"I'll hit him up. I'll keep you posted."

"Let me know. I'll let you know if I hear from him."

Tuesday morning came. I scrolled through all of my messages and texts. None of them were from Bryan. Aaron hadn't heard from him either.

When I picked Bryan up from the homeless shelter the week prior, he made it a point to let me know that he had brought carfentanil with him on the bus from Florida. He told me he was going to save it for a random time. I told him he'd be better off getting rid of it.

Aaron and I both had the same thought as we discussed Bryan being unreachable. We came up with a plan of action for that coming Tuesday morning. Aaron would head to Toledo to meet me at Bryan's apartment. I was going to head from Perrysburg to Toledo. Aaron had an hour and a half drive. My drive was fifteen minutes. We agreed to meet at Bryan's apartment at eleven thirty that morning.

I opened my bedroom door that Tuesday morning and walked through Jane's house to leave. My friend Jane had never met Bryan, but I had updated her on his situation during all those trips to Florida the prior year. I looked Jane in the eyes as I left my room that morning. She knew something was off.

"What?"

"I'll let you know once I find out."

"Are you ok?"

"I am. I'm fairly sure it's about to be a bad day, though."

"What's going…"

"I'll be back in a bit."

I left Jane's house. I was hungry. I had a feeling that if I didn't stop for food, I wasn't going to have an appetite once the day progressed. I stopped and ate breakfast at a fast-food restaurant. I tried to call Bryan again. No answer. I called Aaron from the booth at the restaurant.

"Hey, I'll be there in ten minutes. Just got done eating. I'm leaving now."

"Ok, I still have forty-five minutes to drive. I'll see you then."

I pulled up and parked on the street in front of Bryan's

apartment complex. I racked a cartridge in the chamber of my handgun. I walked to the door, my finger resting ever so slightly on the trigger of my nine-millimeter. I flicked off the safety with my thumb as I approached the door.

The front door to the apartment building was unlocked. I opened it, and I scanned from left to right and back again. I walked to the left to reach Bryan's front door. I knocked twice. I rested my left hand over my right hand on the gun's grip. I waited a few seconds. I checked the door handle to Bryan's apartment. The handle turned. The door was unlocked. I pushed the door open as I held my gun down at my side. I walked in...

I took a deep breath. Keeping my head on a swivel, I called out Bryan's name. No response, just silence. I saw the bathroom light, it was on. I stepped through the living room in that direction. I saw something out of place as I approached the bathroom.

As I stepped into the open bathroom doorway, the vision already in my head suddenly played out in front of me as well. I stood there, just a second longer. I knew I had to clear the rest of the apartment. I quickly moved into the kitchen, my gun raised in front of me. The kitchen was clear. Bryan's phone and wallet were on the kitchen counter. I put Bryan's phone in my pocket.

I quickly walked back to the opposite side of the apartment. I moved into the hallway, past the door to Bryan's bathroom. I opened the closet door. The closet was clear. I stepped into Bryan's bedroom. I looked all around. I checked under the bed. The bedroom was also clear. I lowered my handgun and walked back to the bathroom. It was only four steps to the open doorway. The light was on...

I crouched down in the doorway. I reached out my hand. I put my hand on my friend's shoulder as he sat there on the floor...leaning towards his toilet. I looked into Bryan's face. I told him goodbye. Silence was heavy in the air. It weighed me down to the floor next to my friend. I felt my eyes well up. I slowly shook my head. I was as ready as I could have been for that moment, yet it burned into me just the same.

I hung up the phone. Aaron was ten minutes from Bryan's apartment. For some reason, Aaron sounded surprised when I told him what I found. He knew that situation very well. His brother had been found in a similar fashion as a senior in high school. Bryan and I were seniors when Aaron's brother overdosed in his house. Aaron, two years younger, was then left without his brother.

Aaron and I hugged. We hadn't seen each other in years. It felt like a lifetime. I had drugs and a gun on me. We decided Aaron would be the one to call the police and handle the scene from there on out. I left. I threw Bryan's phone from my car window into a creek as I drove back to Perrysburg. I hoped someone would do the same for me if it ever came to it.

Back at Jane's house, I informed her of what I had just seen. I called my sister...and then my ex-wife. I notified other lifelong friends. I made sure people kept the news off of social media. I knew Bryan and his dad weren't on speaking terms, and they hadn't been for a long time. I wanted to be sure Bryan's dad found out through proper channels, not social media whispers and rumors.

I managed Bryan's death as I always handled losing loved ones. I skipped all the typical steps and went directly to acceptance. I felt slightly envious. I wanted to rest. Why wasn't I able to rest like Bryan? My daily life continued unabated. My mind, still slipping.

Bryan was a relic from my past life. In a way, he was what I needed to let go of to fully transcend into the abyss. I lost my family when I lost my mom in 2011. She had held everything together. I let go of basically all family ties as the years progressed beyond her passing. I lost my own life partners with failed relationships since I began dating in high school. My career was over as of May 2018. My home, no longer my sanctuary, no longer existed.

I stepped into 2019 by taking my first step into homelessness. Through all the changes, Bryan was one lifelong friend who remained close. When Bryan left the world, he stepped away from me. I thought that, in a way, I may have actually died with my friend.

Pariah Carry

"Alright, she just texted. She's out in the parking lot."

I handed Kevin a bag. I then handed Kevin a handgun. Kevin put the bag in his pocket and the gun in his waistband. He walked out of his apartment, leaving me alone inside. About ten minutes later, he walked back in. He gave the gun back. I put it back in my ankle holster. Kevin then handed me a stack of bills. I counted out his finder's fee and added the stack of money to the other stack in my pocket. Our system had worked.

I made sure none of the business we conducted had me involved in any aspect around any houseguests. Kevin was happy being the plug to his friends. He liked being the plug to his associates when the scene suddenly dried up due to a citywide sweep south of his apartment. By the end of that day, Kevin and I came out well ahead.

The entire week followed that day's template. Kevin was a bigshot to all his friends. Sometimes, girls came inside to hang out with the two of us for a little while when they showed up to score. The girls were genuinely impressed with his image as the new plug. The girls liked me, too. They found me charming. I was the cute friend, there hanging out while Kevin conducted business.

...

A year prior, I was still in corporate America. It was spring of 2018. I had one more sixteen-hour day at work until I was off for three days in a row. I needed to be in my office at five in the morning on the days I worked. It was an hour commute to my workplace. To make it on time, I had to leave for work by four in the morning. That meant I needed to wake up at three fifteen every scheduled workday. On days I worked, I didn't arrive back home until well into the night.

With crystal fueling me, most nights I chose to stay awake when I worked…awake for up to six days in a row. The extended time awake sometimes caused me to sleep through my alarm when I did get sleep. Exhaustion, on those nights where I would crash, resulted in negative consequences when I overslept.

I knew I only had one more day of work. I knew I was about to have an unprecedented three days in a row off work. That night back in 2018, I decided I was going to livestream on the website the entire time I was home to keep myself from crashing. Not sleeping would prevent subsequent oversleeping and showing up late to work. I wanted no problems before the upcoming three-day reprieve.

I was still living alone in my big empty house, and it was a rare night where I didn't have company. I livestreamed from my living room. I responded to my audience as they sent comments to me while I was naked in front of my camera. My goal was to finish before I needed to leave for work.

Hours went by with an audience watching me on the website. As three o'clock approached, my situation became more urgent. I was pouring sweat and exhausted, both physically and mentally. I was sore. I was frustrated. Three o'clock came and went…four o'clock passed by as well. I should have left at four o'clock to make it to work and unlock my department by five o'clock.

My audience cheered me on. Women sent me pictures and videos of themselves naked to help me reach climax. Amazingly, five minutes after four o'clock, I finished on camera, to the delight of all my viewers. I wanted to cry, I was so frustrated. I wanted to sleep, but I couldn't. I was physically and mentally spent, and I had no time left for a reprieve.

I had to shut off the livestream, quickly dress, and rush to work. I didn't have time to shower. At that point, I didn't care anyhow. Tired and stressed, I made it in time to start up my department, just as my first wave of employees walked in to begin their days.

My mind had already checked out of the corporate world, though my body remained at my job for another few months. I spent that first part of 2018 living in the new internet hookup world on my phone as the company world crumbled around me at work.

I checked my phone once my department was up and running for the day. I sat in my office as I read all the new messages on my phone, messages which I received in response to the livestream. Almost all of the messages were typical compliments and requests to meet. One message stood out from the rest.

A girl named Shelly had seen the livestream, she had actually only seen the final two hours of it. There were no compliments about my appearance or my sex appeal in her message. What she wrote, instead, was exceptionally deep and very personal.

"I saw the desperation and pain in your eyes as you tried to finish. I hurt for you. I felt something inside me as your pain danced with my own…"

Shelly then shared a story with me that made me hurt for her. Something had happened to Shelly two years prior. It left her traumatized to the point where she hadn't left her home at all for two years. Shelly was twenty-five years old, and the incident had left her in her parents' care that whole time, because she couldn't care for herself.

As my workday progressed, Shelly and I interacted with one another. We texted. I talked to her on my phone while I was in my office. We exchanged voice notes as I walked the factory floor. Shelly and I bonded in a strange and immediate way. By the dark of the evening, Shelly chose me to be her reason to finally begin to rebuild her life. She wanted me to pick her up and bring her back to my house. She wanted to share thoughts, experiences, and intimacy with me.

"I feel like I was meant to come pick you up today."

"I feel it too. I'm scared to leave my house, but I know

you'll help me through my fears."

Shelly wanted to try all which she could think of once the two of us arrived at my house. She wanted to make videos. She wanted to try crystal. She wanted me to guide her into intimate closeness and share moments of erotic beauty.

"That was one of the best orgasms I've ever had in my entire life."

The words barely escaped my lips. I collapsed backward from my knees to my bedroom floor. Ten hours had passed that first night I shared with Shelly. Her naked body soon lay in my arms. We both slept right there that next morning, cuddling on the bedroom floor by my walk-in closet. Once we woke a few hours later, we did more drugs. Shelly made a request.

"I wanna stay here with you the next three days...until you have to go back to work."

The only time during those three days with Shelly when the two of us weren't naked was when we went for a drive through the farmland around Perrysburg. I showed her the power of the car audio system in my car.

"I've always loved bass. I had a good system in my car in high school."

"Well, I'm warning you...I put a lot of work into this..."

"I can handle it."

The bass was too much.

"Pull over. You have to pull over."

Alongside a corn field on a country road just south of Perrysburg, I pulled my car to an abrupt stop. Shelly barely opened the door in time. The bass caused her to vomit, right there on the road. As I looked on, I felt a strange sense of pride. The work I had put into my audio system had proved legit.

The last night during our first weekend together, Shelly decided she needed to finally sleep. I tucked her in my bed, and I walked out to my living room to livestream on the website. I had an idea. I wanted to try out the idea in front of an internet audience.

I moved one of my couches into a position in front of the web camera in my living room. People began to join the online audience once I began the live feed. I stripped fully naked. I positioned myself on the couch and began.

Sleep-deprived, I fell asleep almost instantly. I woke up seven hours later. I was still on the couch. I was still naked and livestreaming. Not only was I still in front of a then larger audience, but I also saw line after line of comments from people laughing at my ridiculous predicament, snoring on camera and sleeping naked, upside down on a live video feed.

Seven hours of sleep...seven hours of viewers tuning in and out to catch a glimpse of the absurdity. Seven hours, and one lady from Australia watched me the entire time. That lady also sent me thirty-two private messages as she watched me sleep. That livestream began a weird period of trans-continental cyberstalking. It wasn't until two months later when I was finally able to shake that situation back down under.

...

A year later, I was content with the week I spent at Kevin's apartment, playing plug-by-proxy. At the end of that week in 2019, I left Kevin's apartment for a short minute to meet Shelly at a large sporting goods store. She was driving again by 2019. She had slowly integrated back into the world outside of her house. I was happy for her. The two of us had remained friends.

I greeted Shelly, and we walked inside. We ate at the restaurant on the second floor of the store. She and I conversed as we each ate our sandwiches. I smiled across the table to her.

"I did really well this week...I'm thinking of buying a BMW."

After I decided to buy a BMW, I found one I liked on a social media market. The owner was in the Indianapolis area. The two of us agreed for me to come down to buy the car that upcoming weekend. I had the rest of the week to take a final trip in my current vehicle.

I had tried to begin my life of travel with a trip to see Kelly in 2018. It didn't happen. I again let Kelly know that I was on my way to see her. It had been a full year since my car had stranded me on my third attempt to drive to Kentucky. Kelly had since apologized for accusing me of being a demon. I still owed her a visit. I had a do-over.

I started my car. I set a zipped-up case of supplies on the passenger seat next to me. I thought for a second. I forgot my backpack of extra clothes. I hopped out of my car to head back inside Jane's house for my clothes. I shut the car door.

"NO!"

My hand wasn't quick enough. The door closed. My car keys and my drug bag were locked in my running car. I heard the faint sound of the car stereo through the glass of the windows. I saw the exhaust smoke rising from the tailpipes. I shook my head.

I still had my phone in my pocket when I walked up to Jane's front door. I knew I had just locked the door, so I knocked. Jane opened the door with a confused look, and I told her what just happened. I stepped inside the house, and I called the police station.

"I don't suppose you have an officer able to come break into my car for me. I locked myself out."

"It's a slow day. Someone could probably stop out."

"Well, it's running. The sooner the better."

"It'll be about fifteen minutes."

After the officer managed to work his way into my car, I was ready to try to leave again. I hopped in and left Jane's house. It seemed as if I wasn't supposed to make it to southern Kentucky to see Kelly that time either.

I was only two miles down the country road in Perrysburg when I stopped at a red light. As I sat and waited for the light to change, a car missed the red light and plowed into the side of a girl's pickup truck at full highway speed. Both cars ended up in a ditch. I stepped from my car to help. Both drivers involved in the crash were conscious and lucid. They both climbed from the ditch with minimal help from others on the scene. I made sure my help wasn't needed, and I continued my departure from Perrysburg. I turned onto the interstate ramp five minutes later. I then made the overdue trip to see Kelly in Kentucky.

I woke up on Saturday in my room at Jane's house. Each thousand-dollar stack of bills was wrapped separate with hair-ties. I needed another two thousand dollars, so I visited my bank. I was closer, but I still needed five hundred more. I had to wait a little longer. I had a solution; the customer service department at Kroger opened soon. There was a Western Union at the Perrysburg Kroger.

Two days earlier, I had arrived back from Kentucky, and I spent that night up in Michigan at my friend Steve's house. Steve taught me a lesson before I traveled to Indiana to buy a BMW.

"Looks like I'm gonna come up five hundred short for the car."

Steve looked up at me.

"Well, that sucks."

"I told that to my friend Greg just now. He offered to cover it."

"Take it."

"Dude, I can't just take money like that."

"I'm gonna tell you something I learned from my dad."

"Ok..."

"Do you feel happy or sad when you give someone a gift? You feel happy, of course. Do you offer gifts to others which hurt you to offer? No, you give gifts to others which won't affect you negatively. Would you rather know your gift is helping someone you care about, or would you rather they refuse your gift and continue to struggle? Of course, you'd feel better seeing that your gift helped the person you care about instead of seeing them refuse the gift and go forth needing the item they refused to accept from you. Take the gift. It'll make you both happier."

"Honestly, I never thought of it like that before."

"Seriously..."

"Alright...I'll text Greg."

I felt weird about it, but I went to Kroger when the customer service department opened. I fed the employee the required information, and I collected that final five hundred dollars. I then drove down to Indianapolis.

My current car was at a point where I didn't trust it anymore. I removed all the speakers, the amplifiers, the head unit, the upgraded wiring system, the line converter, the capacitor, and the upgraded battery. My drive down to Indianapolis was silent.

I agreed to leave my car as a trade-in along with payment for the BMW. Paxton was going to meet me at his dealership.

"Hey man, I'm a half hour out."

"Alright, hey...I need to head back to my house. Can you meet me there? I'll send you the address. It'll save you from having to drive through the city. My wife needs to go to work. I need to watch the kids. I'll have the car and paperwork here. "

"Uh...yeah. That's fine..."

I pulled my car into Paxton's garage. I made sure all my items were with me as I closed the door and handed Paxton the keys. That car was then his. Paxton gave me the key fob for the BMW. We took the car out for a test drive. He handed me the service records and the bill of sale. Paxton went to hand me the title. He paused for a second.

"Oh, man. This is a title for a different car. Well, you have the bill of sale. I'll send you the title as soon as I get back to the dealership tomorrow. That works, right?"

I handed Paxton the stacks of money. I hopped in my new car and drove away. I had a temp-tag as a license plate. I had already switched my insurance to the BMW. I was good to go.

It was a fun drive back to Perrysburg. I arrived back at Jane's house later that afternoon. I showed Jane and her kids my new car. Jane was impressed it had only taken me a week to go from mentioning I wanted a BMW to having one. I walked to my bedroom. I began to interact with a friend of mine in Columbus.

"Well, I got that car today. I can head to Columbus tomorrow."

Clem & Geraldine

I had a girlfriend when I was twenty years old, during a time when I lived in a party house with four of my friends. Sarika had been a grade behind me in high school, though I didn't know her until she showed up at one of our house parties. She arrived at the party with a friend of hers, one whom I had been sleeping with.

Sarika and I remained friends through all of the following years after we dated. The two of us sometimes indulged in unique and experimental intimacy. We created moments and memories unique to our dynamic.

Though I was happy to continue to randomly experience our wonderful lovemaking, Sarika put a stop to the sexual aspect of our dynamic prior to 2019. I respected her and our friendship, so our then-platonic friendship continued.

In 2019, Sarika moved to an affluent suburb of Chicago. We made plans for me to spend a few days with her in Chicago on my return trip from Oklahoma. It was my first trip to Oklahoma. It didn't go as planned. I was ghosted two out of three times while there. I blew a tire in Oklahoma city, and the engine of my BMW switched into low power mode on the drive back. I didn't know what that meant, but my car was running rough. I needed a few days with Sarika to decompress.

I made it to Sarika's house in mid-afternoon. We embraced at the front door. I looked into my friend's eyes.

"What's wrong?"

"I'm fine…you said you needed to shower. Come on, follow me."

Sarika took me to her favorite fancy Chicago hotdog restaurant. She took me to multiple Mexican food locations, and to her favorite ice cream shop. I left her house, on occasion, to make other planned stops while in Chicago. Each time I returned from my little side adventures, she was eager to show me more of her favorite new spots in her new city. As we relaxed in her living room one evening, I remembered something.

"I wanna show you a video. You'll like it. You'll laugh."

She looked up at me.

"It's from Athens, Ohio the other week. I had to do it to earn a badly needed shower. I was driving back to a friend's house in Columbus from a girl's house in Chillicothe and randomly connected with someone with an interesting fetish."

Sarika laughed a little to herself. "Show me."

I smiled at her. I decided to send her the video.

"Check your messages."

I watched Sarika as she watched the video.

"Oh, my God! You...are ridiculous!"

We both laughed. I was happy to see her laughing. Since I first asked her what was wrong when I showed up at her house, Sarika had a strange, distant, and distracted demeanor. I didn't push the issue, but I assured her that she could tell me anything without judgement. Because she hadn't brought it up, I decided I would do my best to make her smile and laugh while I stayed at her house.

Sarika had a lynx cat as a pet. The cat was cute, and he was huge. The cat continued purring when I stopped petting him. I stood up and grabbed my bags. It was time to leave. Sarika was headed out of town for work the next morning. I was headed to Findlay, Ohio to see a friend. I dreaded the drive between Chicago and Toledo, a boring and drab stretch of road, similar to the drive between Toledo and Cleveland. I wanted to get it over with.

Sarika and I hugged, and we said our goodbyes. I walked to the door. As I opened the door, Sarika broke down crying. I stopped, I heard my friend behind me. I shut the door again. Sarika, overtaken with emotion, could no longer hold back whatever it was that was bothering her. I rushed over to her and put my arms around her. I settled back in, ready to listen. I was there for her. The drive to Findlay was put on a back burner.

...

Adrian left for work, leaving me alone on his couch in Findlay, Ohio. Adrian managed a few hours of sleep before he went to work. I hadn't slept. I did crystal to keep going. The previous night, I had stayed late in Chicago to comfort Sarika. I had been doing extra hotrails to compensate for the boring drive from Chicago. I just kept on going harder once I reached Adrian's house. The sun had risen. It was morning.

I planned to quit doing drugs and get a bit of sleep as soon as Adrian left for work. I would have done just that, but I was fairly sure I was about to have to save a friend of mine up in Michigan. I was having trouble sorting out the details of what was going on with her, but I could see, in the video calls, that my friend Betsy needed help.

I had originally met Betsy in the 1990s at the Perrysburg skate park. My Perrysburg friends began including her in our exploits during our high school years. My friend Aaron lost his virginity to Betsy as I sat next to the two of them on a basement couch in 1997. Betsy had also known Bryan and his brother, Alex. When I found Bryan dead in his bathroom, Betsy heard the news from me. Betsy had been lost to me for years, but we had been back in contact again after my second marriage ended. We hadn't seen each other in person in almost two decades.

Betsy looked distressed and scared during the video calls. Her wild eyes were darting in every direction. Her pupils were black saucers, filling the entire colored parts of her eyes. She would whisper that she needed help, and then the call would suddenly end. A few moments later, my phone would ring again. Betsy would be in a different room for each video-call. All the rooms were dark behind her. All she managed to tell me was that she was not alone, someone else was there sleeping.

After about three hours of sporadic video calls, I was finally assured Betsy was in no immediate danger. She sent me the address. She was in Michigan. I told her I would come pick her up, but I had a long drive ahead of me. I was an hour from the Michigan border. Betsy was another hour up in Michigan. I texted my friend Adrian.

"Hey man, I have to leave. I'll lock up. Get a hold of me later on."

While I was on my way to Betsy, my phone blew up with calls. It was Angie. Angie and I had barely been in contact in 2019. I let the calls go to voicemail, I already had one estranged friend to worry about. My phone rang one more time. I answered the call. Angie had been arrested for erratic driving.

"Listen, you gotta pick me up before shift change here. They're gonna leave me in jail over the weekend. They said I can get a ride out of here right now."

"I'm already on my way to help someone else..."

"Please! They're gonna keep me here!"

I sighed.

"Alright...I need directions, or an address, or something."

Angie had to put the sheriff on the phone to explain directions to pick her up. I was familiar with the city, but I hadn't been aware of the location of the police station. The sheriff gave me the address, and I put the coordinates in my GPS.

"Ok, it shows I can be there in an hour. Thank you, sir. I'll see you then."

Betsy was blowing up my phone with calls the entire drive. I answered right after I hung up with the sheriff.

"I'm still coming, I promise. Something else came up. I'll be there. It'll just be later on."

Betsy blew her top. She yelled and cussed at me. I hung up on her. For the next hour, I continuously declined calls from Betsy as I followed the directions to reach Angie. I was annoyed with her pestering.

Once inside the police station, I spoke with the receptionist. She directed me to have a seat. I sat in the lobby for about ten minutes, and then a door opened.

"Doug?"

I stood up in response, and I followed the officer down a hallway. The officer held a door open while I walked through. The officer followed. We were then standing outside.

"Doug...I'm really sorry to tell you this. Right after I got off the phone with you, Angie's probation officer called here and told us she needed to be left in jail. My officers found a bunch of contraband in her car. We were still planning to let her go with a summons and a court date, but our hands were tied after her probation officer called. I'm really sorry for the inconvenience."

I shook the sheriff's hand.

"I hope this somehow helps her. I've honestly been worried about her lately. Hopefully, somehow this is a good thing."

I walked back to my car. I knew Angie was in a downward spiral. We hadn't talked much in 2019. I had cut her off. Her money was no longer good in my eyes. Anytime I talked to Angie, I advised her to get help. The two of us had grown apart after we stopped making videos together when I first joined the website. I couldn't help her destroy herself with drugs.

I drove away, and I stopped at the first rest stop once I reached the highway. I thoroughly searched my car for any planted tracking devices. I knew crystal made me paranoid, but I wasn't taking any chances.

I drove into Michigan and picked Betsy up from the address she had sent me earlier. That day, Betsy switched from crack to meth. It was never my goal to start anyone on crystal. If someone didn't do drugs, I kept my drug use to myself. If someone wasn't already looking to get zooted, I never pressured them to get high with me. If someone wished to try crystal, I was fine with it...as long as it was their decision. The situation with Betsy was unique.

I had been deep into all drugs at one point or another for

two and a half decades, since my early teens. I hadn't had crystal in my life until I was thirty-seven years old. From the first time I used crystal, I fell in love. Though I knew Betsy wasn't going to kick any drug habit in my presence, I was sure she would be better off on meth than she had been on crack.

Betsy was so deep into the crack rock that my only option was to offer her crystal. Betsy wanted me to take her to get a rock. I set her up with a hotrail of crystal instead. As we drove the backroads of Michigan, she quickly forgot about wanting crack. She calmed down. She chilled out. She sat back against the passenger seat of the car. I began to understand her words more clearly. Betsy's come-down from crack was replaced with a much longer-lasting stimulant.

Saddle Point

By May of 2019, Kevin and his girlfriend, Sasha had broken up. Sasha no longer lived in Kevin's apartment in Downriver. Some nights, I left Kevin's place to meet Sasha at a shopping center, her mom's house, or some random location in the Detroit metro area. Though the two of them were not together anymore, both Kevin and Sasha still had the habit which introduced them to me in the first place.

Kevin and I were hitting it hard during one of the later weeks in May. Kevin had taken an optional layoff from work. He and I were tweaking hard and barely sleeping. The revolving door of Kevin's friends kept business booming. We were overstimulated.

There were times I would throw crystals at Kevin from another room. They would sometimes bounce under the stove or the refrigerator. There was one day when I lost one of my ounce bags of crystal somewhere. The two of us combed Kevin's house for two hours. I suddenly remembered where I left it…it was in my car. After Kevin bought a quarter of the bag from me, Kevin lost his bag of crystal. Two more hours of searching the apartment, and all was accounted for.

When I left to meet Sasha at a Walmart, Kevin locked himself out of his apartment. When I returned, I went over to a neighbor's house where Kevin was hanging out. After an hour at the apartment, Kevin found his keys. They were in his pocket.

Kevin and I were both sleep-deprived and mentally compromised. We came back from a party one night, and I tripped on the cement curb. As I was walking in from the parking lot, I fell on the cement outside the door to Kevin's apartment. The fall caused me to hurt my arm and land on my phone. The phone still worked, but it was cracked.

Kevin was normally a calm guy, but sometimes too much crystal made him paranoid. He'd become convinced that his house was going to be raided by police. When Sasha was still living with Kevin, she used to text me when Kevin grew paranoid and flushed an eightball or a quarter down the toilet. I kept Kevin's drugs in my own pockets whenever I stayed at the apartment to keep his drugs out of the toilet.

Kevin was well into his paranoia one afternoon. The two of us hadn't slept for a few days. I had a solution to Kevin's mindset. I told Kevin that he should lock up, and we should take a trip on the Blueridge Parkway to Asheville, North Carolina. Kevin checked all his windows and grabbed some clothes. We were ready to walk out the door. We didn't walk out the door for another two hours...I had lost my keys.

Three days later, Kevin and I drove through West Virginia in the middle of the night as we headed back up to Michigan. Kevin had eaten more crystal at one time than I had ever seen anyone eat. It was two thirty in the morning, and I had no clue where we were. All I knew was that we were in the mountains. We hadn't seen any signs for a gas station, and our fuel situation had become urgent. I finally exited the highway. I had to try something, we were about to be stranded on the interstate. When I pulled off the highway, I drove directly into a horror movie.

Still on the exit ramp, Kevin and I looked down to the other highway below us. There was a pickup truck on the road. It was parked on the shoulder. Three Mexican men, dressed as cowboys, walked in each of the lanes on the highway below. The Mexicans walked together, side by side, and they were all scanning the highway with flashlights.

I continued driving on the overpass exit. The road turned to the right as it reached a flat cliff face on the side of a mountain. There were no lights above the street. There was no light anywhere, aside from my headlights.

After five more minutes of driving in the mountain darkness, the two of us noticed that we were approaching some sort of buildings. The buildings appeared to be homes. When we reached the start of the structures, we were fully aware that the whole area was like nowhere we had seen before.

The dark mountain road opened up to a grid of residential streets. The homes were shacks, or worse. Some of the lots had remnants of what were once structures, now just piles of debris. Tents were pitched in some of the lots. Run-down campers and buildings with tarps replacing walls; the farther in we went, the creepier the scenery. We both felt uneasy. We both hoped the fumes propelling my car would keep us going until we were through to the other side.

That was when Kevin saw the first one. I saw her a second later. On the side of the road, walking in the same direction we were traveling, was a prostitute. She was walking as if in a stupor, like a zombie. As I caught up to her in my car, I looked over at her face. She never turned her head. She never acknowledged the car as it passed right by her. Her face was reminiscent of a zombie. Her glazed-over eyes stared blankly ahead. Her sunken-in cheeks and pale skin startled me as I passed her by.

As soon as I put my eyes back on the road, I noticed someone else walking in the opposite direction a hundred feet ahead. It was another lady of the night. She too seemed oblivious to anything going on around her. Her walk was slow and stiff, her gaze fixed straight ahead, to nothing. The feeling I had building inside me was growing worse. I looked at Kevin. He looked at me. Neither of us said a word. I knew Kevin was feeling the same way I was. I saw it in his eyes.

The BMW crept through that little village in the middle of the night. As more of those night walkers came into view, I thought about how I couldn't wait to be anywhere else at all. In my mind, I begged my car to keep running. I wished to see a gas station. I prayed to make it through that nightmare location deep in the mountains of backwoods West Virginia.

Time passed silently and slowly. I watched the night-walking ladies fade out of view as I passed through the last of the grid. Two minutes later, the lights of a gas station appeared up ahead. Five minutes after that, Kevin and I were back at another ramp on the interstate. We were ten miles away from where those Mexican men had been combing the road with flashlights below our original exit from the highway, but we were finally back on the interstate.

As the sun began to light the sky later that morning, Kevin and I crossed into Ohio. We still had a day until Memorial Day Weekend, so we decided to spend that entire Thursday at Hocking Hills. Kevin had always wanted to visit. I hadn't been there since my friend Sarika took me on a trip for my birthday a decade prior.

Situated in Logan, Ohio, southeast of Columbus, Hocking Hills State Park is a jewel in the southern Ohio landscape. Hocking Hills boasts twenty-five miles of some of the most beautiful and naturally breathtaking hiking scenery in the entire country. Wooden bridges and steps link sections of trails which wind through cliffs within a forest. Waterfalls and caves line the gorge where a clear and pristine body of water trickles its way through the center of the ravines.

Inside the entirety of the park, visitors feel isolated from the world beyond the forest. The land has a magical quality, reminiscent of a fairy tale, a fantasy world of nature. Southeastern Ohio between the lateral line through Columbus and the border with West Virginia, is a lush, forested land of rolling hills and mountainous regions. Hocking Hills, the pinnacle of the southeastern Ohio landscape.

Kevin and I entered the park from the south. I parked the car in the small lot by Cedar Falls Trail. As music came through the car's speakers, we passed the silver tray back and forth. We sat with the doors open as we blew down hotrails. The smoke dissipated in the air of the park.

I unstrapped my handgun and placed it under my seat. I emptied paraphernalia from my backpack, and I threw a couple of unopened water bottles into my bag. It was mid-morning. Though there were some stray storm clouds, the sun was mostly shining that morning. The temperature was already well above eighty degrees, but I assumed the shade from the forest would provide relief from the intensifying heat of late spring. We were ready to explore the beautiful area.

Kevin and I walked down the wooden steps to the base of the gorge. The basin at the bottom of Cedar Falls was beautiful. The light-blue water was clear, and the rocks and gravel at the bottom of the pool were colorful. The fish were easy to spot as they swam lazily in the water. A brown rock face circled the pool of water a hundred and eighty degrees. The forest which lined the water, lush and green. In the middle, directly across from where we stood, was Cedar Falls.

Cedar Falls poured over the top of the rocky cliff face. The water hit a location on the side of the cliff and created a tier before the second cascade of water fell into the tranquil pool below. The sound of the falling water echoed throughout the gorge. The entire location was stunning.

Keven crossed over a wooden bridge, and he wandered out of sight downstream. I remained on the rocks at the precipice of the waterfall basin, along with some randomly scattered hikers. A family of four explored the overhang which jutted out over the right side of the pool of water. A woman to the left of the falls recorded video of the flowing water with her cellphone.

I stood at the very edge of the rocks, directly across from the waterfall. I positioned myself on a slippery rockface, one with a wet mossy surface, due to the mist in the air from the waterfall. As I recorded video with my phone, I took a step to the right to capture a different angle.

As I took that step, I slipped on the wet moss underneath my feet. My legs shot out from under me, toward the pool of water. As I fell into the pool, my right shoulder and arm came down hard on the rocks. So did my head. My right hand, still gripping my phone, hit the corner of a rock where the drop-off to the pool began.

Before I knew it, I was off the rocks and plunging into the water. Both my shins hit the same jagged rock below the tranquil surface of the pool. Then, I went under. My right leg twisted as I reached the bottom. My ankle twisted even more as the rest of my body finished the descent to the gravel and sediment submerged below.

Instinctively, I shot back to the surface to stand up as soon as my brain caught up with my fall. The water, once I was again standing, reached my armpits. My right arm immediately shot out from the pool, still grasping my phone in my right hand. I reached up to gently toss the phone back up to the dry section of the rocks above, and I saw blood on my elbow. I saw more blood coming from my hand. I plunged my arm back into the water.

With my left hand, I pulled my wallet from my left pocket. At the same time, I reached my bleeding right hand into my right pocket and pulled out a soaking wet wad of a thousand dollars. I tossed both items up onto the rocks where I tossed my phone.

I caught my breath, and I adjusted the glasses on my face. They managed to stay on my head through the fall. I looked around and began to take inventory of all the places I hurt. I had a headache from smacking the back of my head on the rocks. My right arm wasn't dislocated, but I could barely move it at my shoulder. I had cuts and scrapes all over my body. I looked down into the clear water and saw blood drifting in the slow current, away from both of my shins, just below my knees. I tried to take a step...I could barely stand on my right leg.

Even had I not been injured, the rocks were a good two feet above my head as I stood in the water...and they were extremely slippery. I wasn't going to be able to climb out of the water at the same spot where I fell in. I looked around. Nobody was close. Nobody had seen it happen. I figured I would be able to leave my phone, wallet, and cash up above me on the rocks while I waded farther into the pool of water.

The bottom right side of the pool, below the rock overhang, was a gradual slope of multi-colored gravel. The gravel eventually reached the surface of the water at the point the overhang shaded the pool from the sun. I hobbled towards my right as the water gradually became shallower. By the time I staggered to where I was only ankle deep, both of my shins were red from blood trickling down from around my knees.

I limped across the rocks at the edge of the pool to where my items had been tossed. I lay down on the flat rock surface as I put my wallet and money back into my pockets. I was soaking wet and bleeding from both legs and from my right arm. I looked at my phone. The corner of my phone screen had broken away. The bottom third of the screen had cracks throughout. Somehow...the video was still recording.

I laughed to myself as I groaned in pain. I shut off the video and put my wet head back onto the rock. I lay there in the sunny spot on the big flat rock. I closed my eyes. When I opened them, I was in Kevin's shadow. Kevin laughed.

"Are you alright?"

I managed to stand up. I regained my composure, but the right side of my body was in constant pain. Kevin didn't take me seriously. He kept rushing me to hurry up so we could hike. I somehow agreed to hike the trail away from Cedar Falls. The trail was uneven and narrow. I sometimes had to catch myself with my left arm as I fell past a tree so I wouldn't fall off the edge, down the ravine, and into the river. I hobbled, and I complained.

An hour later, it began to rain. It was slippery everywhere. I struggled forward. Kevin went ahead, and I eventually caught up as he sat waiting on a rock. Kevin went ahead again.

That pace continued for hours. I became increasingly irritated and exhausted. I had one hour of sleep two nights before that and had been awake ever since. I had been driving most of that time. I was exerting energy I didn't have as we were hiking in Hocking Hills. I was using half of my body to traverse steep inclines and declines over rocks and slippery mud. I was attempting to climb over trees and plants in the woods while not slipping off the side of the cliffs and down into the gorge below.

For three miles, I struggled to keep up with Kevin. We finally made it to Old Man's Cave. It was raining. My phone battery had been dead for some time. I was amazed the phone still worked at all.

I reached the point of giving up at the base of the stairs which led to Old Man's Cave. I could go no further. There were people everywhere in that part of the ravine. The main entrance to the park was so close, yet it was up at the top of the gorge. I was at the bottom. There were multiple flights of stone stairs carved into the sides of the cliffs. There were multiple flights of wooden stairs which led out over the center of the gorge, and to bridges back-and-forth at various levels of elevation across the ravine. Finally, there was the hike through the cave itself, a steep incline which had been made slick from the continuing rain.

"Just go. I can't walk anymore right now."

I knew the final trek would be my most challenging. I didn't need Kevin around to annoy me. I sat for what felt like a lifetime at the base of those stairs. Hikers passed me, headed both directions. Finally, I stood up and decided it was time to go. The rain kept increasing. I just wanted the ordeal to end.

It was another long stretch of time before I made it past the different flights of stairs and bridges crisscrossing the ravine. I reached the entrance to the amphitheater-like dome of the cave. Hikers; college kids, families with small children, and even the elderly were passing me by. Some asked me if I was all right. I waved them off. It was dry in the cave section of the inclined hiking trail. I sat on a cold rock and lay back onto it. The cold felt good on my legs and back…then I fell asleep.

I didn't know how long I slept. I was sure the smiles on the hikers around me were due to my snores echoing throughout the large cavern. I was fairly sure one of my snores had been what jolted me awake. I sat up into a sharp pain which shot up the entire right side of my body. I hobbled on through the cave, toward the top of the gorge.

As I stepped out from under the rocks, rain poured down from the sky. There weren't many people outside anymore. The ones who remained were all running towards their cars in the parking lot. I had that same goal in mind. I just couldn't run. I reached the parking area. Nothing looked familiar. That entire hike hadn't been a loop around the whole park. It had been a three-mile hike to the opposite side of the park. It had been a three-mile hike away from my car.

I felt defeated as I stood there alone in the rain. I pressed forward. I came upon the entrance of the main campground as I stumbled down the side of the road. In the distance, I saw a sign for guest services and a medical building. I made it to the door of the building. I hobbled in, soaking wet and bleeding, and I walked up to the front desk.

"I need help."

I agreed to file a report to initiate medical treatment. My injuries were looked over, and I was bandaged up. I couldn't call Kevin. My phone was dead. The park employees let me borrow a charging cord, and I plugged in my phone while being treated. When I called Kevin's phone, it went straight to voicemail. Kevin's phone had died as well.

A park ranger showed up. There was no way I could make the three mile walk in the rain on those treacherous trails in my condition. By then, thunder and lightning were hitting hard as the rain had become a severe storm. The ranger helped me to his truck and sat me in the back. I closed the door. The ranger talked to me through the dividing cage as he drove me through the forest to the other side of the park. We drove around for a while looking for Kevin. When we didn't find him, we decided the best bet was to drop me off at my car and hope Kevin finds his way back.

"The park's closing in one hour. A night rescue here is not an ideal situation. I hope your friend shows up. Best of luck."

"Again, thank you. I never would've made it back without you."

I had no way of physically looking for Kevin. I was

debilitated and completely spent. I sat in my car and did hotrails. All I could do was wait. About forty-five minutes went by, and all of a sudden Kevin jumped into the passenger seat. I told Kevin what had happened to me. He then told me how his time had gone since we separated earlier in the day.

When he reached the top of the cave earlier, Kevin had also thought he was at the parking lot where I was parked. Once he realized he wasn't, he turned back to try to find me. He couldn't find me though, because I was asleep on a rock in a cave. After Kevin abandoned that idea, he wandered around in the parking lot and looked for someone to give him a ride to the other side of the park.

Kevin met a young couple. They said they would give him a ride. They told him they had their car back at their campsite down the road. Kevin had been awake and tweaking as long as I had, and he had done more crystal. He hadn't remembered if the couple told him to follow them to the campsite or to wait for them in the parking lot.

After deciding to follow the couple to their campsite, Kevin chose to remain a bit back from them due to being unsure if that was what he was supposed to do. He lost sight of the couple. He then wandered in an arbitrary direction. Kevin remembered being in a clearing in a field on the side of an unfamiliar road. He remembered waking up after sleeping in that field, feeling rested as the thunderstorm thoroughly soaked him with rain. Somehow, Kevin managed to find his way back to the correct parking lot. His phone hadn't died...there just wasn't any cellphone service out in the forest.

I offered Kevin a hotrail, and he blew it down. We left Hocking Hills State Park. It was still raining. The sun began to set. Kevin was asleep again before I made it to the interstate ramp. He slept the rest of the drive through Ohio and all the way to his apartment in Michigan.

Kevin and I returned from our trip the day before 2019

Memorial Day Weekend was about to begin. Each year, since the dawn of the millennium, the Detroit Electronic Music Festival took place in Hart Plaza in downtown Detroit. It was a three-day music festival which drew millions of visitors and musicians from all around the world.

I had a plan for the festival in 2019. It was the first year I wasn't going to go just to party. I was prepared. I had VIP tickets for all three days of the event. I had people set up to work for me. I was set to network and make substantial amounts of money.

Nope.

My injuries from falling into the water at Hocking Hills changed all my plans. I posted the tickets for sale on an online market forum. I sold the tickets for half their value to a nice Biracial lesbian up in Taylor, Michigan. The two of us hung out for a minute when I met her to give her the tickets. I was happy that she was an enthusiastic fan of the electronic music scene. I drove back to Jane's house after selling the tickets, where I spent the weekend unable to walk. I watched videos of the festival from my bed.

Bass Boost

When I logged into one of the hookup apps in 2019, I saw a familiar face. I sent a message to the Mexican transgender girl in the profile, asking her name. She replied with the name I knew she was going to tell me. I asked if she remembered me. I shared some of the details from our night together almost twenty years prior. Christy filled in the memory with her account of the rest of the evening. She was surprised to hear from me. The two of us caught up with each other for a few minutes. Christy then invited me to her house, a home she shared with her husband.

Though I mostly chose to avoid group sex when the option presented, I agreed to participate in the three-way dynamic. The girl from my past sat in a chair at the foot of the bed. Earlier, Christy had tied her husband's arms to the bedposts as he was lying on his back. She had tied each of his legs to each of his respective arms. He was blindfolded and gagged.

Both husband and wife were big into the party scene. Every once in a while, Christy and I untied the husband so he could join us as we did drugs. After Christy's husband did what she felt was enough crystal, she slapped him in the face a few times and reapplied the bindings. The night became morning. The next day went by with much of that same activity. The couple was thoroughly impressed with the quality of my crystal. My mind was on something else.

"I've been looking for someone to install the new head unit I bought for my car stereo last week. I need to start upgrading the audio system in my BMW. Every business I've tried so far won't touch the complicated electronics. Do either of you know a mechanic? Do either of you work on cars?"

The couple looked at each other. At the same time, they both answered.

"Dan!"

Dan, same as I, had a black BMW. He worked as a mechanic at a car dealership in Lansing, Michigan. Dan had upgraded the stereo in his own BMW. He liked to party as much as they did. Christy sent a text message. Moments later, he replied.

"I'm off at six. I'll be over by six thirty."

That was my cue to take a break from the dungeon-like scene and take a shower. I was sitting on a chair in the bedroom later that evening when Dan walked in. Dan and I were instant best friends. Our humor was the same. Our taste in music was the same. Our taste in cars was the same. Our drug of choice was the same. We were the same age. We shared favorite movies and television shows, which we quoted back and forth between us the entire evening. Dan and I even finished a few of each other's sentences.

I told Dan of my desire to upgrade my car audio system. We made plans to begin working the next week at Dan's place of employment once the dealership closed for the day. We agreed on a form of payment which made sense. Dan liked to party, and I could bring the party to him every day we worked on my car.

I felt my phone vibrate in my pocket. I checked my messages. I gathered up my belongings, and I left Christy's house. I returned the missed phone call on my way to Downriver.

"Yeah, I've got you covered. I'll be there in an hour. Dude, Kevin...I think I found someone to help me with my car stereo."

The following afternoon, I left Kevin's house. I had to make a couple stops in Detroit. I was just two exits away from Kevin's place when my car began to overheat on the highway. I pulled off the interstate at the next exit and parked in a shopping center. My car was dripping coolant all over the pavement. I added coolant, and I immediately contacted my mechanic in Perrysburg. I warily drove down to Ohio to wait for my mechanic to show up at his shop.

My mechanic showed up with his newly hired assistant.

The assistant, Jose, was twenty-eight and lived in Toledo. As my mechanic worked on another car at the shop, I rode with Jose in his pickup truck to run some errands. He needed to pick up some parts from a dealership. He needed to stop and get money from a bank, and he needed to run a personal errand. I sat in the truck with Jose in the parking lot of an apartment complex.

"Heroin dealers are always late."

"My guy's usually on time. He should be here any…there he is right there."

When Jose and I arrived back to the shop, my mechanic showed me the leaking water pump on my car. He then searched online for anywhere selling that particular water pump. One was found for sale at a parts store in Sterling Heights, Michigan, a suburb just above Detroit.

"Go ahead and take my truck. I'll catch a ride home later."

I left my car in Perrysburg and headed to Michigan in Jose's pickup truck. Ten minutes after I left the shop, Jose called my cellphone.

"What's up?"

"Do you wanna save some money and get your car back quicker?"

"How's that?"

"Once you get the part, bring it back to the shop tonight. I'll meet you here and do it myself."

"Sounds good to me."

I stopped and picked up Kevin on my way to Sterling Heights. Kevin wanted me to swing by a check-cashing store so he could get a cash advance on his paycheck. Kevin needed crystal. His friends had almost run him dry that day while I was in Ohio. I stopped so he could go inside and get a cash advance. He came back out and handed me a stack of money.

By the time I picked up the water pump and dropped Kevin back off at his apartment, I heard tornado warning sirens. The clouds rolling in were black. I stayed just long enough to do some hotrails at Kevin's place. I knew I needed to hurry and get the pickup truck back on the road. The storm was moving in fast.

The storm hit as I passed through Monroe on the interstate. The sky was greenish black all around me. The rain came down so hard and fast that everyone on the road dropped their speeds to a crawl and turned on their blinking four-way hazard lights. I drove, white-knuckled, as the sounds of the storm overtook the radio in the pickup truck. Cars were suddenly in the median and off the sides of the road. I pushed on, agonizingly slowly, as I tried to avoid hitting stopped vehicles and traffic in the lanes around me.

Suddenly, the entire highway came to a stop. The rain ceased. For a split second, the sky was eerily calm. It was black outside. The air was silent. All I could see were the flashing lights of other stopped vehicles around me. A moment later, the intensity of the wind and rain picked up. The black sky consumed all the lights from the other vehicles, and Jose's pickup truck began to shake. It felt like I was about to flip over. A black nightmare wall of sky passed across the highway in front of me from the right side to the left. The noise was deafening.

As soon as the apex of violence in the air had passed, there was again a moment of stillness and silence. The silence was broken when hail began to fall with the rain. The sound of the ice hitting the metal and glass all around me was again deafening. Cars began to move. I barely saw those lights of the cars directly in front of me.

I weaved in and out of traffic as I tried my hardest to maintain control against the wind, rain, and hail. Jose told me he would be waiting for me at the shop in Ohio. I maintained myself through a tornado. I then tried to maintain myself on the road the rest of the way out of Michigan. Sections of the road were flooding fast.

I reached the shop in Perrysburg. It was still pouring rain. The gravel lot between the buildings of the complex was full of huge puddles of water. I saw the shop; the lights were off. I jumped out of the pickup, and I was instantly drenched as I looked through the windows of the overhead bay door. As the rain poured down on me, I shined a light from my phone into the shop. My BMW wasn't inside.

I jumped back in the pickup truck, and I called Jose. Jose wasn't at the shop as he said he would be. He was out scoring heroin...in my BMW...which was leaking coolant...and also still had the issue which kicked it into low power mode...and it was storming to the point where roads were being shut down from flash flooding.

I was angry.

Jose pulled into the lot in my BMW. I yelled my displeasure as Jose unlocked the overhead door so he could drive the car inside. I walked inside behind my car and pushed the button to close the door. I handed Jose the box with the water pump. I used a few more choice words and told Jose to start working on my car. I sat on a folding chair in the bay next to the hydraulic lift where Jose had raised up the BMW.

"I'm sorry, man. I was just...it took longer than I thought to meet up with my guy. I was originally going to be home and waiting, but he didn't show up when he said he would."

I just sat there, shaking my head as I watched Jose begin to work underneath the car.

"Just get the job done."

That day, I had driven from Michigan to Ohio, and back to Michigan, and then back to Ohio. I had sat in a pickup truck as I waited on a heroin dealer to bring Jose heroin. I had driven through hail, torrential rains, and flooding...and into a tornado, just to have to wait at a shop where I was told someone would be waiting for me.

I was angry.

I then had to find out my car was being driven all over the place in my absence, risking more expensive and inconvenient damage. I had to listen to excuses from the person who kept me waiting. I had to listen to more excuses from the guy who risked damage to my car while driving it to get drugs, in a severe storm, while the car had immediate service issues.

I was angry.

Then, in the space between heartbeats, something

happened which instantly made me forget all prior events that day. In the time it took to blink, I witnessed something I never could have predicted. What I saw shifted my brain and mindset to a place it had never been. In that moment, time stopped completely. I moved timelessly, as did all that was my world around me. In that moment, existence itself froze.

The visual of what happened came first. My eyes sprang wide, as my mouth dropped open. I was, in that moment, frozen. I stood, a statue, as a scream from close-by pierced my ears, echoing resonance through my brain. I wasn't angry or annoyed, I was no longer worn out from the day's activities. I wasn't impatient, wishing to leave in my repaired car. In that moment, I was nothing at all.

As if the Creator himself flipped a switch, all of time and motion instantly started up again…and as I finished that single blink over my then wide eyes, the entire world moved in fast-forward.

Jose had been driving my car during the time I was using his truck to go procure my new water pump. The BMW's engine had been on, and it had been running until just a minute before Jose began working on it. I was sitting in that chair, feeling annoyed, watching Jose as he stood under the front of the car, changing the water pump. I was sitting there watching as he reached up with a wrench to remove a coolant hose from underneath the car.

I was sitting there watching as that coolant hose suddenly sprang loose. I watched as the boiling coolant sprayed directly into Jose's face. I saw the smoke poof out from both sides of Jose's head. I heard the sizzle of the coolant as it hit Jose's skin. I heard Jose scream in agony as he instantly covered his face and fell to the ground…and my shock-paralysis gave way to urgency.

I jumped from the chair and ran to a bin of towels and rags. As I passed by the bin, I pulled out a couple towels. I ran to Jose and dropped down beside him. I had to yell to get through to him.

"Drop your hands!"

Jose's screaming was drowning me out. I physically pulled his arms down to his sides. I wrapped the first towel around his face.

"Hold it there."

I ran, with the second towel, to the bathroom. I turned on the water, and I drenched the towel. I dripped a trail of water as I ran with the soaked towel back to where Jose was writhing in pain on the floor. I wrapped the soaking-wet towel around his face.

"Keep holding it."

I scrambled and found a bucket. I filled up the bucket in the bathroom. Jose's screaming had degraded to moans and shrieks. I ran back to him with the bucket of water.

'Keep the towels there. I'm gonna pour this water on you."

Time passed. Jose calmed down. I sat back down in the chair after I guided him to another chair, one which was pulled up next to mine. I shook my head in disbelief.

"Dude, I'm still annoyed, but I'm not gonna let you lose your face or go blind."

"Thank you..."

Jose explained the process of changing the water pump. I used his tools to change the water pump myself. Jose's face was burnt, but his eyes had avoided the majority of the coolant. I found first-aid cream in an emergency supply kit. Jose was able to help talk me through the repairs after I coated his face with the cream from the kit.

I still paid Jose the agreed-upon amount in the end, though I was the one who changed the water pump. I made sure he was able to drive, and I followed him to the emergency room a mile down the road in Perrysburg. Once he made it inside, I drove to Jane's house to sleep.

Heresy and Conjecture

The week before Dan and I were set to work on my car audio system, I decided to begin the upgrades on my own. Though I planned to let Dan handle the complicated computer system of the BMW, I figured I was able to start on the twenty speakers I wished to add to the car.

The garage at Kevin's mom's house in Taylor, Michigan was in the back yard. The cement driveway ran up from the road, along the side of the house, and through the gate of a chain-link fence. The driveway then opened up to a wide cement platform in front of the garage in the backyard. It was the ideal spot to park the car, remove the seats and interior, and prime the car for speaker installation.

As I backed my car up the driveway alongside the house, I slowly inched my way between the sides of the chain-link fence. When I reached the point where my front car doors were even with the fence line, I heard and felt an awful grating against my car. I had completely caved in and destroyed the driver's side front door of the BMW on the fence.

I was fortunate that Kevin's uncle owned a body shop in the Detroit area. Kevin called his uncle and handed me the phone. I took my car to Kevin's uncle's house for him to inspect. The next day, I took my car to the body shop.

That day, I paid just four hundred dollars. Within a couple of hours, I had my car back. The door looked pristine. I proceeded cautiously when I drove my car through the gate into Kevin's mom's backyard the second time. Kevin and I set up shop in the empty two-car garage. The workbench against the wall became the hotrail station. We used the space along another wall to fill with tools and items from the car. Taylor Tweak Fest began.

I worked on my car compulsively, as I had done with my previous cars. Tweaking gave me a focus which bordered on obsessiveness. Kevin and I didn't sleep. I took breaks in the middle of the night, just so the neighbors weren't weirded out by some guy working on a car at all hours of each day and night. I also didn't want to be noisy with power tools during the hours when others were asleep.

During the nights, I joined Kevin in the basement. Though people would come and go, Kevin and I remained in his mom's basement, blowing down hotrails over and over. Hip-hop music played on the sound system. I interacted online with people from the website. I stepped out, on occasion, for business and pleasure.

...

My judgement lapsed one morning. I let my guard down and agreed to meet someone in Detroit to sample the quality of my product. Though I made sure I let the guy know I wasn't going to show up with any more product than we were going to sample, I still made the wrong choice; I agreed to meet somebody I didn't know and trust.

It was the first time I had agreed to meet a stranger for a drug interaction. I was on high alert. When I found the house, I surveyed the location. I looped around the block and parked two blocks away from the house. I walked down to the house. I only brought one crystal with me from my car. In my right front pocket, I had a loaded semi-automatic handgun.

The side door to the house was in an alcove, at the base of half a flight of stairs. I descended the steps to reach the door. The thug-looking guy opened up the side door. He had tight braids down to his shoulders. He had on a bandana. He was wearing a tank top. I guessed the guy to be in his late twenties.

I walked in. There was a mattress on the floor to the right once I stepped inside the lower floor of the house. There was an old-style television against the opposite wall. Beyond that, there was a doorway. There wasn't a door in the door frame. There was darkness beyond the room I was in.

The guy sat down on one side of the mattress, and I sat on the other. I had no idea if anyone else was in the house. The guy asked me about my product. I reached into my pocket for the single loose crystal. I pulled out the crystal and flicked it to the guy with my thumb.

Surprised, the guy reacted, and he managed to catch the crystal as it was flicked. He turned it around in his fingers as he looked at it. I watched as the guy inspected the chunk of happiness. The guy looked up at me. He nodded. I nodded back, our gazes remained fixed. Suddenly, the guy stood up.

"I'll be right back."

The guy slipped through the doorway into the darkness of the lower floor. I heard him ascending the stairs to the floor above. I stood up with my hand in my pocket, on my handgun. I stepped sideways, towards the door I had come through to enter the house.

I opened the door and looked outside. Nobody was there. I shut the door and locked it from the inside with a deadbolt. I stood with my hand in my pocket and my back against the wall next to the door. My mind raced. I couldn't decide if I should wait longer or run out the door. Suddenly, the guy came back through the doorway.

The guy looked startled to see me standing over by the side door. He looked down and saw my hand was in my pocket. I could see he was sizing up the situation. The guy talked.

"You were right, how you said earlier that you can never be too careful. Here's the truth of what's going on. About a week ago, I got caught with drugs. I now have to cooperate with the police. I have to give them that crystal you gave me. You told me that was all you had with you. When they pull you over as you're leaving, they won't find anything on you. I'm sorry it came to this."

I had been tricked. I walked right into the trap. Though I hadn't brought any more crystal inside the house with me, I did have more in my car. I didn't care about what was in my car at that moment. I had a decision to make.

I had just been robbed. The crystal of mine which the guy had removed from my possession had a street value of just below a hundred dollars. It had a value to me of under five dollars. The guy was also giving me an out. I could leave without shooting him. I had no idea who else was in the house. The sound of a gunshot would certainly attract the attention of anyone else present.

I thought for a second as the two of us gazed across the room at each other. My hand never left my pocket. I conceded the guy's victory. Any option of trying to recover the crystal would require escalation. I wasn't in any mood to catch a case over one crystal. I lost more crystal to clumsiness on a daily basis.

Bravo, I thought as I unlocked the side door and walked from the house. I got caught slipping, and I was separated from my merchandise by nothing more than calm words. The guy earned the payment that day. It was well-deserved.

I paid that crystal to that guy to learn a lesson. I took it to heart. I vowed to never again walk blind into a situation. I vowed to deal with only those people I trusted and knew personally. Things could have gone much worse. The guy got away with a payoff that was well-conceived and deserved. I made it out of there with only losing a gram and a half of crystal. I lost an equal amount to a carpeted floor later that same day.

…

Though Kevin was straight, he had a couple gay friends from high school. One of those gay friends was in contact with him and looking to party. Kevin was happy to make money. I agreed to pick up Ron from his house in Downriver. On the way to Ron's house, Kevin told me what to expect.

Kevin and I pulled up to Ron's house. Ron was waiting outside in his wheelchair. He was bandaged from head to toe. He looked like a disabled mummy. Ron looked exactly as Kevin had described him. Kevin and I helped Ron into the car. We put his wheelchair in the trunk.

Ron was at the end of a relationship, though they both still lived in the same mobile home. Five weeks before I met him, Ron had broken up with his boyfriend. He was distraught, and he decided to end his life. He hadn't thought through the best way to accomplish the task. He chose to jump from the roof of a six-story building to the ground below.

The jump hadn't achieved the desired results. Instead of passing away, Ron broke most of the bones in his lower body and some bones above his waist. He had been on the mend for the prior five weeks. He was also in therapy. Ron told me he no longer wished to die, and he felt more positive with each passing day.

Kevin and I carried Ron into a sandwich shop. After the three of us ate, Kevin and I carried Ron back to his car. I drove the three of us back to Kevin's mom's house. Kevin and I struggled, but we managed to carry Ron down the stairs to Kevin's basement. We sat him down on a couch. I then went back out to my car and brought Ron's wheelchair inside.

The three of us spent the evening doing hotrails and discussing random topics. As the night went on, the drugs kept us going. In the early hours of morning, Kevin and I began to hear weird statements from Ron. It seemed as if Ron's mind was taking him away for a few seconds at a time. We would look over at him as he asked a question to someone who wasn't there. If we asked Ron what he said, he looked back at us silently. Ron then turned back towards nobody and said things that made no sense. The sun rose the following morning,

"Hey man, I'm gonna go work on my car speakers for a while."

Ron insisted he wanted to help. Kevin and I carried Ron up the stairs and put him in the back seat of my car. Kevin went back inside to watch television in the living room with his mom.

After a half-hour of Ron's attempts to assist me with the speakers in my car, Ron wanted to go back inside. It was getting hot outside, and he wished to be on a couch in the cool basement. I retrieved Kevin to help me carry Ron back down the steps.

About two hours passed. I stayed outside, working on my speakers. Hunger soon overtook my thoughts, so I went inside through the back door. I walked through the house to where Kevin and his mom were watching television, and I asked the two of them what food we should order. I stopped for a second to listen.

"Do you hear that?"

"Hear what? I don't hear anything."

"It sounds like running water…"

Kevin and his mom stayed in the living room watching television. I went down to the basement to see what was going on. I walked down the basement stairs, and the sound of running water grew louder as I reached the bottom. The lights in the immediate entertainment room were off, so I didn't see the floor before I stepped down from the bottom of the staircase.

As I stepped from the staircase, I put my foot in two inches of water. I turned on the lights. The entire basement was underwater. The storage boxes and items downstairs were ransacked and strewn all over the place. I yelled for Kevin and his mom to come downstairs. I walked through the entertainment area and turned left at the bar. I turned left again and yelled to Ron to open the bathroom door. I could hear the shower running. Water was flowing out from underneath the bathroom door. Ron didn't reply, so I popped the bathroom door open with a screwdriver from my pocket, one which I had been using outside on my car speakers.

Ron's mummy bandages were floating around everywhere in the water on the bathroom floor. The toilet was overflowing, bandages had been stuffed down into the bowl. I turned the corner to see Ron sitting on the floor of the shower. Water was pouring from the showerhead all over him. He was no longer wearing his clothes. The last of his bandages had been shoved into the shower drain, plugging it up.

The faucet of the bathroom sink had been turned all the way on. The top of the toilet had been removed from the tank. The cleaning supplies from under the bathroom sink had all been pulled from the cabinets. Ron was mumbling to himself about taking some imaginary children to see a movie. He was wearing undergarments: items found in a storage box in Kevin's mom's basement.

Ron had lipstick, blush, and eyeliner smeared all over his face to compliment the bra and panties he wore as he sat contorted on the shower floor. In that moment, I wondered why he needed to be carried everywhere. He seemed fully capable of myriad physical activities.

Kevin and I cleaned Ron up, and we got him dressed in his own clothes. Kevin began to clean up the basement, while Kevin's mom hopped on the phone with her homeowner's insurance company. I took Ron back to his mobile home. Kevin stayed home to help his mom try to shop-vac the water from the basement floor.

Though I put the front seats back in my car, I didn't have the patience to bolt them all the way back down. I spent the drive holding myself, and Ron, in place. Only the front bolts of the seats were secured to the car. At each stop along the way, the back of my seat would lift from the floor and push me into my steering wheel. Frustrated, I pulled off the road and secured both seats with the seatbelts from the back seats.

I helped Ron into his wheelchair at a park a block from his home. Ron's ex-boyfriend walked down to meet us. The ex-boyfriend handed me a laptop computer he brought to the park with him. It was an exchange for something I handed to the ex-boyfriend.

"I promise you…Ron won't do any of this."

I placed the laptop in the back seat of my car and drove away. I saw Ron's ex-boyfriend wheeling Ron down the street as I left the trailer park. I spent a good two hours at Kevin's house deleting all the gay porn from the laptop. Even the background screen was a collage of naked men engaged in various activities together.

As the sun came up the next morning, I was back outside

working on the speakers in my car. I had the car's back end parked in the middle of the garage. The front end was on the pavement in the backyard. I had bought an expensive, high-end amplifier to add to the audio system. I had instantly blown it when I wired it wrong. Kevin and I exchanged the amplifier for another of the same models. Again, I blew it instantly.

Kevin had another project of his own going on. While I worked on my speakers, Kevin took to watering the back lawn with a hose. He wore only a robe and boxer shorts as he watered the lawn for three hours. He also watered the pavement, and the garage, and my car, and my speakers…and he watered me.

When the garbage men came down the street, Kevin finally put down the hose and stopped watering everything in the back yard. Moments later, Kevin's mom ran out the back door to fetch me to come help her stop Kevin from trying to fight the garbage men. His paranoia from being awake too long had extended from an imaginary neighbor (which he tried to point out to me each night, a neighbor who was actually just a lamp post) to the city employees collecting the trash.

That afternoon, I went to a popular taco establishment and bought food for everyone at the house. Kevin's mom had spent the day on the phone with the insurance company, trying to get someone to clean up her completely waterlogged basement. Kevin and I both managed some much-needed sleep that night. We each slept in separate spare bedrooms upstairs; the couches in the basement were no longer options.

The Elephant's Foot

It was hot outside, and I had been doing drugs the entire day. It was only two in the afternoon. I still had four hours until I planned to meet Dan at his workplace. As I approached the Lansing area, I needed gasoline and something cold to drink. I pulled off the interstate to a surface street. There was a gas station just beyond the exit. I pulled in.

As I sat in the parking lot and drank my slushie through a straw, I suddenly felt something in my mouth as it popped between my teeth. My brain flashed instantly to the swarm of fat brown beetles all over the gas station windows and flying around above the slushie machines inside the gas station. I quickly pulled the lid from the drink, and I spit the mouthful of red liquid back into the cup. I looked through the transparent plastic and saw what caused me to spit out the drink.

While I sorted through my inboxes, I read a message from someone who lived out in the country on the northwest side of Lansing. It was an invitation, and I agreed to stop at the house. It was still a couple hours until I could meet Dan. I sent a text with an ETA, and I drove the thirty minutes to reach the house.

Despite other houses dotting the gravel road, I found myself in an isolated country area as I pulled up to the house. The homeowner, dressed as a biker, greeted me at the door. The homeowner's leather jacket matched the multiple motorcycles parked in the front yard. It must have been a pain for a motorcycle enthusiast to deal with nothing but gravel roads five miles in every direction.

From the neck down, the homeowner could blend in perfectly at a biker bar: jeans, boots, a belt with a large metal buckle, a leather jacket, and a t-shirt. From the neck up, the homeowner was more suited for a show bar: long black hair, hoop earrings, false eyelashes, and a full face of makeup.

The two of us sat and talked in the old farmhouse. Mementos and photographs were everywhere, and the furniture looked antique, like family heirlooms. There was no electricity in the house…no lights and no air conditioning. We couldn't sit outside and talk, as the mosquitoes were plentiful and very painful. I was already bitten by at least four mosquitoes as I walked up to the house when I arrived.

"I haven't had power since that storm came through the other night."

As we sat and talked, sweat poured from me. I took off my clothes in an attempt to cool down. I continued to drip sweat everywhere. I wiped myself off continuously. I was fully undressed, and I couldn't cool down at all.

"Can I get a towel?"

As we talked, the homeowner's eyes suddenly brightened. His demeanor changed. It was as if the homeowner suddenly remembered something.

"I have to show you what I've been working on upstairs! You'll love it!"

I didn't think twice about it. I wrapped the towel around my waist, and I followed the homeowner through two cluttered rooms to the stairs. I insisted the homeowner lead the way up the stairs. It was dark without electricity. I wasn't afraid of becoming a victim of a serial killer. I was far more concerned with tripping on one of the steps as I went upstairs.

The old wooden steps creaked and cracked as we ascended. There was a strange alcove at the top of the stairs. It looked like something was missing.

"You ready for this?"

"Um…sure."

As the door pushed open, I saw light coming through to the top of the steps. I figured there must have been a few large windows supplying light to the top floor of the old farmhouse, and my assumption was accurate. Light illuminated the entire upstairs of the house. I walked into a creation which I had never seen before. I was amazed and impressed. I knew my facial expression had not gone unnoticed.

"Do you like it? I've been constructing it for a long time. It isn't done, but here...let me show you around."

The entire upstairs of the house was one large room. There was a vaulted ceiling where the roof came to a high point. Each corner of the area seemed to serve as a special station of its own. The light, which shone through the large windows on three sides of the room, illuminated everything.

The paint was rainbow-colored everywhere. There were rainbow glittery ribbons and ropes strung from all the walls and the ceiling. From locations throughout the ribbons and ropes, there were large bolts in the ceiling and on the walls. The bolts held chains. Some chains ran along the walls. Shackles were at the ends of the chains. Some chains and shackles were suspended and hanging freely above a bed in one corner of the room and above an examination table in another.

There was a sex swing and an inversion table. There were various platforms and support devices. There were chairs, some with restraints and others positioned as if for observation. The quality and work that had to have gone into that immaculate and intricate sex dungeon was nothing short of expert.

"This is amazing."

"I may use the area at the top of the stairs for a sort-of ticket booth."

"What's that door at the far side of the room?"

"Go ahead, open it. Just be sure to step back as you do."

I opened the door. There was nothing beyond the door except the outside. The door opened to a view of the backyard. There was a drop-off just beyond the doorway. I walked to the edge. It was a long drop down to the back yard.

"I'm not sure what I'm going to do with that door, but it has potential."

The homeowner bought that specific house with the

intentions of turning the upstairs into a private sex club for fetish seekers. Construction was almost complete. I was told of a few other items which were still needed to finish out the project: two more sex swings to match the one already suspended in one corner of the room, more whips, more leather, alcohol to stock the bar next to the door to oblivion... I sensed the pride the homeowner felt with each item and section of the room I was shown.

"Can I video the tour of this place?"

"Absolutely."

"This is incredible. I've never seen anything like it. Thank you for showing me this."

I sincerely meant every word. I was genuinely blown away. The entire top floor of the house had been turned into a functional work of art. A vision had come together, and what had materialized was the dream of someone capable of making that dream a reality.

The two of us went back downstairs to the living room when the tour concluded. Though I was impressed, I was far too overheated to try out any of the equipment. I stood naked in the living room as the homeowner sat in front of me on the couch. I remained standing there without pants as I put my shirt and backpack on my unclothed body. As I stepped into my pants, I held them up around my waist. I stood there a bit longer so the homeowner could keep going for a few more minutes. I then stepped back and zipped up. It was close to six o'clock. I was still pouring sweat from everywhere.

"You can stay for dinner if you want."

"Thank you, but I gotta go. Thanks again for showing me that upstairs. I'm impressed."

I walked out into the mosquitoes and made my way to my car. It was hot outside, but there was a breeze. I was still dripping sweat as I pulled from the driveway to the gravel road. I sorted out my supplies, and I did a large hotrail while I drove down the gravel road.

"Everyone's leaving now. Pull around to the back at six

fifteen. I'll open up one of the doors."

I stopped at a fast-food restaurant at six o'clock that evening. The restaurant was on the service road in front of the dealership. I sat in the parking lot of the restaurant and ate my food. At six fifteen, I drove from the parking lot to the back of the dealership.

Dan was standing inside the overhead door. I could see him as I pulled up. I saw Dan hit the button to open the door. He marshalled me into the service bay as I inched my car through the doorway. I turned off my car and stepped out into the service garage. For the next three weeks, I met Dan at the dealership after the rest of the employees went home each evening. Dan worked on my car audio system. I helped on occasion. We did drugs the entire time.

On the evenings when the car audio work dragged late into the night, Dan and I stayed in hotel rooms close to Dan's work. On the days when I was still up to drive, I would leave for Kevin's mom's house to continue my nights over there.

As time ticked away, I knew that Kevin planned to get sober. I had a talk with him about his future plans. That conversation led to Kevin's last night of partying. He and I agreed to stay in touch, but we decided that hanging out was not going to be a possibility. I respected Kevin, and I gave him the space he required to be sober and get his life on track.

During those three weeks, I also had a conversation with Jane about the room I rented from her.

"So I met a lady in Upstate New York. Once my car stereo's done, I'm moving there."

I rented a moving van, and I emptied out my bedroom at Jane's house. I took all my belongings to my storage unit where the rest of my items from my old house were in storage. Jane said goodbye to me. She also mentioned something which I found peculiar.

"I know you're going to New York…but I just have a weird feeling that life has something more for you down South."

What Jane said to me that day somehow made perfect

sense. I looked Jane in her eyes before I walked out the door. I spoke a final thought.

"I think you may be right…"

It was a Sunday when I drove through Lansing, Michigan. The storm clouds accumulated in the sky. The roads were void of traffic. I pulled into the dealership in the late morning. Dan and I got to work. There wasn't much left that needed to be done. I hoped to be on the road to New York by four o'clock that afternoon. The rain hit, and Dan shut the door to the shop. We remained inside the car dealership until the storm passed.

It was four fifteen when I hit the road to New York. I was excited for the new adventure. I anticipated my first physical interaction with a woman I knew online for two months. I was happy to finally take another step away from any kind of normal stationary life in the Midwest. I felt as close to alive as I had in a long time.

Tiptoe Through the Two Lips

As the sky began to turn that pre-dawn purple, I pulled up to my new home. All the lights were off in the house in front of me as I sat in my car in Elaine's driveway. I gathered up my backpack and texted Elaine to let her know I was there. The early morning mosquitoes were as bad as they had been at the sex club house outside Lansing.

I reached the porch, and I set down my backpack. I unzipped it and sprayed myself with bug spray. I had an idea, and I knew I needed bug spray before executing my plan. Elaine hadn't responded to my text. She was still asleep. I waited to call her to attempt to wake her up. I wanted to get ready to make a maximum impact on our first meeting.

The property was huge, and the porch I stood on was far back from the street. Few cars were passing at that hour, and the house far across the street was still dark without activity. I stripped off all of my clothes and stood there on the porch of my new residence. I smiled. It was then that I video-called Elaine to finally wake her up to let me inside.

Elaine was a single White female. She was a generation older than me. She had a quality which exuded classiness and sensuality. Her straight blonde hair flowed down to the top of her chest, and it was all cut to that same length. Her body was elegantly thin, with curves in the appropriate places. She stood 5'6" tall. Had I not known her age, I would have guessed her to be much younger.

I kept my drug use to myself while I settled into my life in New York. Elaine and I braved the mosquitoes and made love amongst the trees and brush deep in the backyard. I did housework and worked on my car stereo once Elaine left to work her job in the daytime. When she came home from work, the two of us drove around the city, frequenting restaurants and ice cream shops. We drove to mountain overlooks to watch the sun as it set above the mountains.

On weekends, I went with Elaine to a mountainside ranch where her horse was stabled. While she rode her horse, I made videos of the scenery around me. Elaine showed me around the area where she had spent her life. We drove into the city. We took trips to the Hudson River.

I wished I felt I fit in. I felt out of place. I felt the same as I had in Ohio, like I was looking through a window to catch a glimpse of a life that wasn't mine. I felt empty inside. I felt bad that I couldn't just fit into the new life, in a large comfortable home, in a pretty new location, with a kind and beautiful woman. A thought echoed in my mind, something about people not being able to run away from themselves...

The drugs kept me going, but my happiness was fleeting. Elaine saw, no matter what...I couldn't be happy. It was the story of my life, but she took it personally. I didn't know how to share my thoughts with her and let her know it wasn't anything against her. I didn't know how to sort it out within myself.

I woke up one morning to a note while Elaine was at work. She expressed sadness in the note. She told me, in writing, that after a month of the way we were living, it wasn't able to continue. I felt bad. I hadn't lived up to her expectations. I did as the note advised, and I left before Elaine arrived home from work that evening.

I was in my head as I drove down the Taconic State Parkway that afternoon. I found a motel and got a room amongst the mountain backdrop of the highway. I walked down the front of the motel to my room. I opened the door and stepped inside. After a thorough bedbug check, I brought in all the bags from my car. I sat on one of the beds after I spread out my belongings on the other and pulled out my phone to continue a text conversation with a Jamaican transgender girl from Poughkeepsie. We had been in contact the prior week.

I had planned to leave Upstate New York that next morning. I planned to stop at Niagara Falls for the fifth time in 2019.

"You can't leave New York until we see each other. Promise me."

"You'll have to come see me tonight."

"Alright. I'll be over once I'm off work. I'll spend the night."

Sharra and I did hotrails on the motel bed. We undressed and began an incredibly unique and long expression of intimacy, one that continued at the motel until the following morning. After a short break while we switched locations that next morning, we resumed once we reached Sharra's top-floor apartment in downtown Poughkeepsie.

Our intimacy at the motel began our checking-off of items from each of our own sexual bucket lists. Sharra accomplished two of the items she had always wished to try. One of those was a first for me as well. I then checked off a bucket list item of my own. Sharra was happy to oblige.

Our drug use and intimacy amplified once we were in Sharra's apartment. Sharra had a balcony and a sunroom outside her apartment. Those spots, along with the rest of her apartment, were used to the fullest. The two of us got high continuously as we remained sexual. In conversation, we shared our individual tastes in music and movies, art, and life.

By the third day at Sharra's apartment, she was beginning to fall out. She didn't have the experience or tolerance which I had with crystal. As she readied herself for sleep, I took a hotrail to the face, one which was so large that the cloud filled up the room. That was when I knew I made a mistake.

The fire alarm in Sharra's building was wired into the fire station of the city of Poughkeepsie. The cloud I had blown out was too much. The light flashed on and off while the warning horn shrieked at a deafening volume. I set off the alarm for the entire building. I also set off the alarm at the Poughkeepsie fire station. I couldn't believe I had done that, and I couldn't believe Sharra hadn't warned me before it came to that.

Sharra dressed to go outside with the rest of the tenants filing out onto the street. I dressed quickly as well, but I remained upstairs and began to put away any evidence of drugs. I sprayed aerosol deodorizer once I stashed the evidence. While Sharra had gone to explain and apologize to her neighbors, I knew, at any moment, the fire department would be coming up to the apartment to shut off the alarm.

Sharra told me the response time to the fire alarm was only five minutes. I knew she was going to try to stall the emergency responders. I knew she had three flights of stairs to ascend with the responders before they entered the apartment, and I knew I had to get every window open on both sides of the apartment to create a cross-breeze to clear out the drug smoke.

The wind, once the windows were open, swept the smoke outside. The aerosol covered the smell of methamphetamine. Sharra and the fire department walked in right after I had done all I could do to decontaminate the apartment. My actions had been enough. After a quick look-around, and after one of the responders turned off the alarm, the fire department left.

We were relieved. Once we watched the firetruck drive away, I breathed a sigh of...another hotrail. Sharra and I both got naked again. We climbed into bed to get some sleep. It had been a long and eventful week. I knew I had a long drive the next day.

I also knew I was still going to make that fifth visit of the year to Niagara Falls. I thought about how I was about to leave what was once a hopeful and promising new opportunity to make a life in Upstate New York...an opportunity I had squandered away like everything else.

Michigander

Dan had been renting a house in Lansing, Michigan. That house transitioned to my new jump-off point in the Midwest once I came back from New York. Kevin was clean from drugs, and I was giving him space. I no longer had any of my belongings at Jane's house in Ohio. Besides my friends, my storage unit was the only connection to Ohio I still kept. Michigan came much more into focus.

I stayed at Dan's house on the nights when I was in the area. So did a multitude of Dan's Lansing friends. So did whomever of my friends I happened to have with me on certain nights. Some nights at Dan's house were tame. Others, not so much.

Though my friend Steve was in the habit of developing an extreme attitude problem with me anytime I wasn't able to stop by his house in Tecumseh, I still stayed some nights over there as well. On other days, I stopped over to Steve's house when I was with Betsy. She and I spent the days making odd sex-based videos while Steve was at work.

Betsy was off the crack and on the crystal. She functioned much better as a tweaker than she had previously as a basehead. She also had the same drug-induced compulsion for constant sexual stimulation I had. Whether we were touching ourselves or one another, our car rides to anywhere involved stimulation. At Steve's house, our activities included all which our imaginations allowed.

I sometimes brought Betsy over to Dan's house. It wasn't as frequent an occurrence as our trips to Steve's house, because Betsy didn't live close to Lansing. I swung by and picked up Betsy if she was around when I was returning to Dan's house from Detroit, Ohio, or Indiana. Every once in a while, Betsy would borrow a car from someone and make the drive herself.

The scene in Lansing was volatile. I never knew what was about to pop off. I drove back to Dan's house one evening to meet someone who wanted to party on a higher level than usual. I was on the interstate between Detroit and Lansing. I passed the last rest stop before the exit to Dan's house. I had been driving for a few hours, and I had been awake for a few days.

The night sky was dark. Traffic had grown dense as I approached Lansing proper. The tired feeling which had been building for days overpowered me. I thought to stop at the rest stop to sleep for a short while. I decided I could make it ten more minutes to Dan's house.

I opened my eyes. Instantly, I jerked my steering wheel. I had fallen asleep at the wheel. The elderly man driving the car in the lane to my left had honked to wake me up when I began to float into the left lane. I slapped myself to help remain awake... I opened my eyes again. It then was the driver of a van behind me who honked to make me aware I was no longer driving in only one lane of traffic.

I made a choice in that moment. I signaled, and I eased my way across the two lanes of traffic to my right. I pulled my car to the shoulder of the road. Traffic flowed by me, and I came to a stop a couple of feet onto the shoulder. I activated my four-way hazard lights, and I turned off the car's ignition. Almost instantly, I fell asleep.

I woke up, disoriented, to a sharp tapping sound on my passenger window. Blue and red lights reflected from my mirrors to my eyes. I shook myself awake and rolled down the window on the passenger side of my car. I tried to pull myself together as I woke from a sleep I desperately needed. In the first seconds of my reanimation, I tried to figure out where I was and what was going on. I spoke.

"How's it going?"

"What's going on? Why are you sitting here in your car? Where are you heading tonight?"

"Sorry about that. I've been driving for a few hours. I realized I was about to fall asleep as I was on the road. I decided to pull over. I thought I could make two more exits. I realized I couldn't."

"Where are you coming from tonight?"

"Detroi...no, Columbus. Columbus, Ohio. I'm going back to where I've been staying with a friend of mine in Lansing."

"We got a call that there was someone on the road who may be in need of help..."

"Yeah, man. I'm sorry. I should have stopped at that rest stop I passed a couple of miles back. From now on, I'll be sure to stop before it gets to this point."

"Next time, be sure you stop at a rest stop if you need rest."

"Yeah, man. That's exactly what I just said to you."

"Be safe. Have a good night."

"Thank you, officer. You, also."

I checked my phone. Dan had texted and called me, wondering where I was. I replied and let Dan know I was ten minutes out. I apologized to Dan's guest when I arrived two hours later than originally planned. I told Dan and his guest that they had the police to thank for waking me up, or I would have never even made it that night. As tired as I was, I was sure I would have spent the remainder of that night sleeping on the side of the interstate.

There were six people over at Dan's house one evening while I was sitting on the couch in the living room replying to people from the website. I was in a particular exchange of texts with a girl in Grand Rapids, a girl in my typical fanbase demographic.

There were too many people at Dan's house that evening to have any semblance of privacy with a lady. The girl from the website wasn't able to host in Grand Rapids due to a comparable situation on her end. The two of us came up with an impromptu plan for the evening. Grand Rapids was an hour drive west of Lansing, situated on the coast of Lake Michigan. There was a rest stop on the southern side of the interstate between Lansing and Grand Rapids. We picked a time to meet at the rest stop.

As a way to sleep in my car during road trips, I cut out pieces of the mylar windshield sunshades to fit in each of my car's windows. The sunshades completely blocked view from every angle. I always preferred to sleep naked, no matter where I was. The shades allowed me to sleep naked with impunity at rest stops. I could also do drugs in my car without worry of reproach. I could video-interact with others online as I sat in privacy behind the window shades. The shades also gave me privacy with guests inside my car.

People from Lansing were over at Dan's house frequently. Some, such as I, stayed for prolonged periods of time. Though I was the only person Dan considered a housemate, it wasn't uncommon for others to stay a week or more. Some friends would stay there in between tenures at other locations. Some friends would just party and binge until they couldn't handle it anymore…they would disappear for a short while before starting all over again.

Dan had a Black transgender friend named Tammy. Besides me, Tammy was the closest to another roommate at the house. She had been released from prison in 2018. Her husband was still locked up. Tammy was a smart person. She wrote poetry and stories. She was active in various social issues. She spoke about deep and important topics…and Tammy, like most of the rest of us, partied daily.

I fell asleep on a chair in the living room late one night and suddenly awoke sometime later to Tammy's face an inch from my own. Startled, I pulled my face away from hers in shock.

"What the…?"

"Hey, I have something for you. Let me get it."

I sat there confused as to what caused me to wake up. Tammy handed me a few small items from her purse. She gave me two fidget spinners and a bracelet. I was even more confused. Tammy's attempt to change the subject from what had caused me to wake up had failed, but I thanked her for the items anyway. I did a few hotrails. I decided I had slept enough that night.

One morning after waking up in a hotel in Detroit, I began a dynamic with a beautiful Black transgender girl. She was petite, about 5'5" and 115lbs. She had long straight black hair. Her face was stunning, her body elegant. The two of us agreed for me to pick her up from her house in Lincoln Park, Michigan, a suburb of Detroit.

I put the location in my GPS, and I drove to wait for Sophia to come out from her house. About ten minutes passed, and Sophia hopped in my car. I began the drive from Detroit to Lansing. Sophia told me she did crystal on occasion. I pulled out the equipment, and we began doing hotrails on the drive.

As I exited the highway in Lansing to head over to Dan's house, I had two grams of crystal in a pile on the little silver tray in my center console. I had previously broken up a crystal with a mortar and pestle, so the powder was as fine as confectioner's sugar. I took a turn on the road too quickly, and the powder dumped from the tray to the floor around my gas pedal. I took that as a lesson. Soon afterward, I put Velcro strips on the bottom of the tray and on the leather of my center console.

Sophia sat facing me, on my lap, as we kissed on a couch. Dan instantly had an attraction to Sophia. Dan kept trying to show her his sex toy collection. Sophia got weirded out a little bit, so we chose to leave Dan's house. Sophia and I went to eat. We then picked a hotel in the Lansing area, and I booked a room.

My intimacy with Sophia that night was comprehensive. We engaged in acts which she suggested she wished to try. We utilized the bed and the shower. The two of us fell for each other that night. Crystal fueled us into the early morning. We each managed a couple of hours of sleep as the sun came up. When we woke up in the hotel bed, Sophia lay on her left side as I did the same. She was behind me. For the next twenty minutes, I took her eleven and a half inches.

Sophia and I stayed together for the entirety of the next full week. We did crystal and drove around the state of Michigan. We had sex in my car in Flint one day. We stayed together in my car in a parking lot of a Walmart in Jackson, Michigan another night. We booked hotel rooms in Detroit and Kalamazoo. We decided, at one point, to drive down to the Toledo area.

Sophia and I explored the parks in the Toledo area in the beautiful weather that week. Providence Dam, Oak Openings, and Sidecut were all hiked. I recorded videos of our journeys through nature. We held hands and kissed. We did hotrails in my car. We drove back to Sophia's house the next week, and I dropped her off.

The Dirty Side of a Storm

I was three days into a sleep-deprived tweak late one night at Dan's house. I was zooted hard, and I was losing my desire to be surrounded by a bunch of other tweakers. I decided to go on a road trip, I just wasn't sure where I wanted to go. I left Dan's house and drove to a rest stop slightly east of Lansing. I considered heading over to my friend Lee's house in Holland, Michigan until I could decide where to drive. Then my phone rang.

Since the time Zoe and I first shared that weekend of her pageant together in Cleveland, I had been down to southern Florida to see her one time. Pressing business up North cut that trip short. Zoe and I decided, during that visit, that I was going to come and live with her in southern Florida. Late that night, as I sat in my car at that rest stop, I got the phone call from Zoe. She told me to come to her, so I left immediately.

After leaving the Lansing rest stop, I stopped off at my storage unit in Ohio. The morning passed as I sorted through my belongings in my storage unit. I managed to fit a sixty-inch flatscreen television in my car. I removed the front passenger seat of my BMW, and I left it in the storage unit. It was a move which allowed me to take quite a few more bags of my belongings with me. I emptied and loaded the contents of both of my safes as well.

I had my briefcase with me at Zoe's house in Florida. The entire briefcase was filled with crystal. I set myself up at Zoe's glass dining room table. My briefcase, my silver tray, my pipes, and my torch filled the space on the table in front of me.

Zoe and I made love nonstop for the first week I was there. We drifted apart quickly, though. Zoe slept in her bedroom. I mostly fell asleep on the couch in the living room…when I actually slept. When Zoe was home, she spent most of her time in one of her dressing rooms towards the back of her house. I stayed at the dining room table when I was at the house. I could barely keep up with the dating apps while I was in the Miami area. The women were thirsty, and the notifications kept me busy at all moments of each day.

A month went by, and I could tell the situation at Zoe's house had degraded the same way as my dynamic in New York. The day came when I knew it was time to leave. There was no note to kick me out. Instead, I was the one who took the initiative to break the tension and begin the process of separation.

Liam, a friend of mine from the Midwest, had been living on the coast in Titusville, Florida for almost a year by the time I was leaving Zoe's house in 2019. Titusville was close to Cape Canaveral. It was mostly a lazy little retirement city where people came to live in campers and cabins and spend their twilight years kicking back on the shores of the Atlantic Ocean.

Liam already told me to stop and stay with him for a bit anytime I was in the Florida area. I took three trips back and forth from Miami to move my belongings from Zoe's house to Liam's cottage in Titusville. I managed all three trips over the course of one full day. On my last stop at Zoe's house, I left her a few grams on her refrigerator door to thank her for the hospitality. I hung the bag there with a refrigerator magnet. Zoe and I had a talk before I left her house that final time.

Liam was a needle user. For the week I stayed with him, I went back to my old ways of shooting the crystal into my arms. One day while Liam was at work, I received a message on a dating app from a girl who lived in Kissimmee, Florida. She was a year older than I and very pretty, but it was what she said to me that made me know I had to see her.

Sarah began her messages to me by expressing how it was meant to be that I was in her life. She wrote me poems. She expressed all sorts of emotions which most people would find abnormal. I was all for it. I felt it instantly. I couldn't wait to meet her. We shared all of that, and it was the first day we had been in contact. I knew I was in for a wild ride, and I anticipated and welcomed any interaction between us. I made the drive the next day to her house, which was a few miles away from Disney World.

I had long accepted that I had mental issues by that point in my life. I had always known, and I knew it had some influence on my feelings as I went through life, feeling detached from reality. I never felt I was a regular person. I always enjoyed meeting others who felt the way I did. Those people allowed me to connect and bond over a similarity. Those people seemed to feel some of what I felt. Most of them also understood my attraction to drug use.

I pulled up to Sarah's house in a subdivision behind a large gas station off the main strip in Kissimmee. I saw her car in the driveway. It was packed full of more things than mine had been when I moved down to Florida. The car had four flat tires. Sarah came out front to meet me in her yard.

"My mom has emphysema. She's mostly in bed all the time. Before we do anything, she needs us to go through my stuff in the garage and throw things away."

Sarah was a self-admitted hoarder. Sarah's mom lived with her at the house. Her mom had been on her case about the storage shed on the side of their house.

"That shed is completely full, too. So is my storage unit. We just need to do the stuff in the garage today. You have to be the one to throw things away. Don't even tell me what you're tossing out. If you do, I'll try to stop you."

Sarah took me by the hand and led me from the garage once I helped her decrease the hoard. She talked about all kinds of things as she walked me all the way to the other side of her neighborhood. We made it to a creek with a viaduct. I asked her what we were doing. She told me that we were going to have sex underneath the road, because her mom was awake at her house.

The two of us went down onto the cement below the road. The creek flowed beneath us as cars passed above. Sarah began to undress. It was then that I noticed the large wasp nest right next to us. I told Sarah we needed to find some other place and she agreed. We climbed back out from beneath the road.

There was a set of train tracks above the viaduct which ran parallel to the street. The two of us began to walk amongst the palms and the trees along the tracks. The road split from the rails gradually. The farther along the tracks we walked, the more secluded the area became.

Sarah and I found a small clearing beneath a group of palm trees. There was some sort of factory on the other side of the tree line. We could hear the commotion. We could see dump trucks and cement mixers as they passed a couple hundred yards from us. At that point, neither of us cared. We each began to quickly undress as we kissed.

I felt like the luckiest person in the world as Sarah wrapped her naked body around me. We kissed passionately as I pushed her up against a palm tree. I dropped to my knees, and I buried my face between her legs. Moments later, I was inside her as we lay on the ground. We switched positions a couple times as I thrusted into Sarah. We both were soaked in sweat and covered in plant material.

Sarah led me back to her side of the neighborhood once we both put on our clothes. We walked to the gas station in front of the subdivision before heading back to her house. We both got ice cream to help cool us down. Once back at the house, she led me inside to her bedroom. The air conditioning in the house was a drastic improvement from the hot and humid evening air outside.

Sarah convinced her mom to let me stay and watch movies in the bedroom. She shut the bedroom door. The two of us blew down some hotrails. Sarah put on a movie for background noise so her mom wouldn't hear anything we did in the bedroom. We both stripped again. I sat on the floor by the bed. Sarah faced me and straddled me. We spent the rest of the evening kissing, talking, and gazing into each other's eyes. I stayed inside her the entire time.

"My mom would never allow someone to stay over."

"Hopefully, I'll be back soon."

"Well, I'll be right here."

I walked down the driveway to my car. Sarah walked back inside her house.

The Rippin' and the Tearin'

I drove in the dark through the Florida countryside back to Titusville. I stayed at Liam's house that night. Liam and I shot drugs, and I explained my day with Sarah. The next morning, I left Florida.

I took A1A north and recorded videos of the scenery on the coast. St. Augustine was beautiful. The majestic old buildings, the ornate homes, the ocean…I loved it all. I had a plan, but I had time to stop as I made my way up the East Coast. My first stop was in Savannah, Georgia.

In the summer of 2018, months before that Thanksgiving when my friend Makayla took care of me when I overdosed on heroin, I first met Makayla's girlfriend. Her name was Allison. Allison looked a lot like Makayla, only Allison was White.

Makayla and Allison were trapping out of a hotel room in Toledo. I picked them up and took them back to Makayla's grandma's house so they could get a few more outfits. I dropped the two of them off again at the hotel across town once they were satisfied that they had enough clothes to get through the night. I agreed to pick them up at checkout in the morning.

Allison first tried crystal at my house that next morning. The remainder of the day was based around sex. The two girls began in my living room. I was then invited to join in. The three of us made our way back to my bedroom. Four hours later, I tapped out. I got dressed, and I walked back out to my living room. The two girls dressed as well.

Once the girls sat down on a couch in the living room, their clothes came off again, and they were back at it. Of all the videos I recorded that day, my favorite was one of me walking by my couch while fully clothed, shaking my head at the stamina of the two girls still pleasing each other on the couch.

By 2019, Allison had been living in Savannah, Georgia for half a year. She invited me to stay a night with her when I left Liam's house in Titusville. I drove north, along the Florida coast to Georgia. I pulled into Allison's townhouse complex at two o'clock on a sunny and hot afternoon.

Allison and I caught up; we ate food and did hotrails in Allison's dining room. Allison showed me around some of the city. I spent time with her in her backyard, and I met her boyfriend when he arrived home from work. I was exhausted from driving after yet another extended period of time with no sleep. Allison showed me to the guest bedroom. I slept better that night than I had in a long time. The next morning, feeling refreshed, I continued my drive north along the coast. I had another stop to make before I reached my destination.

While I had been staying in Miami with Zoe, I began a dynamic with a girl who lived in Wilmington, North Carolina. She was a nineteen-year-old Black girl I had met on an app on my phone. She was kind, and shy, and a pleasure to interact with. The two of us hit it off from the start, and I told her I would love to see her when I left Florida. We texted, we talked on the phone, and we video-called each other. The girl's demeanor warmed my heart. She was the person I wished to hold in my arms and keep safe. I kept her updated with each stop on my trip to her from Florida.

It was dark outside that evening after I left a house in Virginia. Hours went by as I drove. I pulled into Wilmington. It was late enough at night that I was the only car on the road. Ziah talked me through the city to her neighborhood. I parked on the side of the street and made sure she had room to sit in my car, full of my belongings. A few moments later, she walked up and got in.

I took Ziah to a hotel for the night after we picked up food. I told her that, besides doing my laundry at the hotel, I was completely hers for the time we were together. We kissed. We undressed one another. Ziah shyly told me she wanted to feel my mouth between her legs. I made her climax as my mouth made love to her body.

The previous autumn, sex with Jay had become the first (and second) time I had orgasmed from anything other than my own hand during the entire 2018 year. After those two orgasms, there had been just two other times where I climaxed literally at the hands of another. Missionary intercourse with Ziah that night in North Carolina in 2019 gave me just the fifth orgasm which my hand hadn't caused since 2017. After all that time, and after all the sexual activity which had taken place back to, and before, when I first found internet meeting sites…and from finding notoriety on that first website, Ziah had done what had only occurred four other times up to that point.

I held Ziah close to me as she drifted to sleep once we ceased our sexual interaction. I cuddled with her and stroked her shoulder softly with my hand. Periodically, I kissed the top of her head. With her head on my chest, she slept the rest of the night in my arms. I got up only to switch over my laundry. I brought Ziah breakfast in the morning, and I felt genuine sadness as I dropped her off back at her house. Before she stepped from my car, Ziah and I agreed that there was more for us in the future.

…

Two days before Halloween in 2019, I drove my way back to Ohio. It was close to midnight when I finally made it through all the construction and lane closures on the Ohio Turnpike just west of Cleveland. I was back on my least favorite stretch of road. The amount of orange construction barrels and closed lanes that particular night only added to my annoyance.

I continued a full half hour beyond the last visible orange sign before I felt relief. The construction was finally behind me.

On my very next breath, one of my tires blew out. My white knuckles gripped the shaking steering wheel tightly. My speed began to drop, but I had to continue driving in the lane I was in for a moment longer. I was on a bridge without a shoulder. When I was finally able to stop, I was between the cement barricade of the bridge and a hill which dropped off into a ditch.

The police showed up and set up flares behind my car. An officer managed to reach a tow truck driver he knew personally. I had to wait an hour and a half on the side of the road for the wrecker to show up, but I received a discount for the twenty-mile tow to the parking lot of an unopen Walmart.

After the tow truck disappeared into the night, I took it upon myself to change my tire in the parking lot. I chose to drive on the donut instead of waiting for the service shop to open six hours later. The lug nuts were rusted on, and I got a serious workout changing that tire. That process took me two hours longer than it should have.

I took a break from driving at an Ohio Turnpike rest stop just east of Perrysburg. I did drugs as I sat in a parking space with a police cruiser behind me and another, three spaces to my right. I was completely spent, and I didn't give the situation a second thought. It worked out, though. Nobody looks for someone in plain sight.

Around mid-morning, I left the rest stop and went to the tire shop in Perrysburg. I had to buy two new tires, because another tire's tread was worn down to nothing. After waiting for the tires, I left and drove to my storage unit. I unloaded my belongings from my car, except the few bags I kept with me on my travels. I then drove to Michigan, to my friend Steve's house in Tecumseh.

I made it the hour drive to Tecumseh and pulled into a gas station. I got gas, and my car refused to start. I tried everything. I checked all the parts I could. I looked up possible issues online. I talked to any mechanic I knew. Nothing. my car was completely dead.

The owner of the gas station happened to be out by the gas

pumps talking with a customer on the other side of the pumps. He noticed I was stuck.

"I need you to not block the pumps."

"Well, my car won't start."

The owner helped me push my car across the parking lot to a parking space. I took the bags from my car, and I walked the mile to Steve's house with two suitcases and two backpacks. I was exhausted when I reached the house. I collapsed inside on a bed.

I checked on my car throughout the weekend. It remained in the parking space at the gas station. When Monday morning came, my friend Amber picked me up from Steve's house. She had AAA, and she offered to have my car towed the hour and a half to Dan's house in Lansing. Amber and I approached the gas station. My car was no longer there.

I walked into the gas station. The owner of the gas station was present, but I didn't see him right away. I was too busy aggressively questioning the worker behind the register. The owner came up to the front of the store. I couldn't believe my car was gone. It had sat all weekend without issue.

"Where is it?!"

"It wasn't us, I promise. Come with me."

The owner led me outside to the side of the building. He pointed to the sign on the fence. "Unauthorized Vehicles Will Be Towed at Owner's Expense."

"Try that phone number. They must have gotten it overnight."

"Thanks..."

I walked back to Amber's car and called the number. Sure enough, my car was towed...to a tow yard thirty minutes west of Tecumseh. I was mad, and I vented my frustrations to Amber as she drove me through the Michigan countryside.

"That'll cost you two hundred and fifty dollars."

"Are you kidding me?! You shouldn't have towed my car!"

"Well, why were you parked there?"

"My car broke down!"

After I mentioned my car had broken down, the animosity in the clerk's voice dialed back a notch. I filled out the paperwork and handed over a stack of money. I let the lady know it was going to be a minute before the tow truck showed up to tow my broken car from the auto yard. I thanked the lady for taking my ransom money, and I went back outside to wait for the tow truck with my friend Amber.

Three hours passed from the time Amber called the tow truck until my car came down off the flatbed in Dan's backyard in Lansing. I was still annoyed with the situation. Dan and I went inside, and I tossed down a large quantity of crystal onto my tray.

"We're about to set some hotrail records."

I tasked Dan with the car repair job. He accepted the challenge. Little did I know, I was in for much more than I bargained. I ordered parts. A fuel pump, some gaskets, a starter, some sensors, the costs accumulated quickly. My car sat immobile. I ordered more gaskets. I bought another battery. I tried replacing a different pair of sensors. My car refused to run.

I spent two weeks as a prisoner at Dan's house without a car. Part of me was fairly certain Dan had planned that situation. I supplied drugs daily. I ordered food daily. Dan came and went as he pleased, while I was sequestered at the house. I had a feeling something was off. The more time that went by, the more frustrated I became with the whole ordeal.

Dan assured me that he was doing all he could to get the car up and running. I was paying Dan in drugs for the labor hours he put into the car, yet I wasn't seeing any results. I began to notice late-night trips outside to the car. I would see other vehicles pull up and pull away within a couple minutes. I was curious if my car was being parted out under my nose.

Round on Both Sides, High in the Middle

Lex, a friend of mine who grew up around the block from me, was a grade below me during our school years, and she hung out with many of the same people I did. Lex had been living in Manhattan for over a decade by 2019. She and I had been in contact frequently since I had previously stayed in Upstate New York.

Lex knew the issues my BMW had been giving me. She helped me fund some of the repairs. When I let her know that the BMW was beyond repair and dead in the backyard at Dan's house, Lex encouraged me to look for a new car. When I found one, I let her know.

Lex sent me the couple-thousand-dollar difference between the money I had and the cost of the car. Dan agreed to drive me from Lansing to Cincinnati, Ohio to buy my next car. I decided, since I failed with the least reliable brand of car, I was going to buy the most reliable brand of car. Lex helped me buy a Lexus.

Dan and I pulled into the dealership in Cincinnati. We checked out the car. Dan went with me to test-drive the Lexus around the city. I had found my next vehicle. It was an IS350. It was black. It was sporty. It drove and handled well. Dan left to drive back up to Lansing. I stayed to finish the paperwork. I made sure I received the title with that car. Once I finished with the formalities, I drove my new car north from Cincinnati.

I had a connection in Dayton, Ohio. Melanie was a twenty-five year-old White transgender girl. Melanie and I would have sex in her room while we waited to score drugs. I always took her somewhere different to meet up with people she knew. The people we met were always different. Melanie knew a lot of people in the crystal scene. I happily paid her a finder's fee to pick up my drug of choice whenever I was in the area.

I stopped to see Melanie in Dayton the night I bought the Lexus. I drove her across the city in my new car to a particularly bad neighborhood on the opposite side of town.

I had basically lived in the Dayton area for six days a week during my tenure working for a company a few years prior. I had lived in the Dayton area with my friend Bryan for a year when I was nineteen. I had many friends and associates throughout the Dayton area. I knew, on that night in November of 2019, I had just driven to the worst possible part of the city.

Melanie had taken me to see yet another group of her friends whom I had never met. We entered the house. Two girls and two guys were inside. The plan that night was for Melanie to stay in the house while I took one of the guys on a run to pick up crystal.

Flip had an entire face full of tattoos. Some of the tattoos were indicative of the time he spent in prison. He had just won a fistfight outside his house before Melanie and I stopped over. Flip's knuckles were bleeding. He wrapped them in a towel. Flip's girl's phone rang. When she hung up, she told Flip that he was good to head out. I left Melanie and her three friends at the house. Flip grabbed a meat cleaver. He said he needed a weapon, and he told me he was ready.

I learned that not only was Flip wanted by authorities for a murder, but he was also wanted by a rival set of a street faction for a retaliation hit, one which he and some associates had pulled on someone two days prior. There was a warrant out for him. There was also a hit out for him. Though I told Flip the meat cleaver was most likely a futile weapon if it came down to it, I never let him know about the nine-millimeter handgun in my pocket. I didn't know if Flip planned to use his weapon to try to separate me from my money, so I took comfort in the ace up my sleeve...in my pocket.

That entire night became a seedy drive through seedy areas of the city. On our first attempted stop, Flip identified an op waiting to attack him. I drove off before we even pulled in front of the house. We made another stop on the side of the road in a subdivision in the middle of what seemed like nowhere, an area just outside of downtown Dayton. We waited there for an hour.

From the beginning, Flip was beyond paranoid. He questioned me about my affiliations. He questioned me to see if I was law enforcement. He continually asserted his love for, and history of, violence. With people on both sides of the law looking for him, Flip seemed to have justifiable reasons for his paranoia.

As we sat in my car on the side of the road in the middle of the night, I believed I gave Flip a sense of reassurance that I wasn't associated with any of the people looking for him. Had he intended to use the meat cleaver on me, he seemed to have reconsidered once we spent all that time talking. Flip was convinced he would be dead, one way or another, in the near future. I convinced him that I was not anyone who sought that result.

After hours in my new car, Flip's phone rang as we sat waiting on the side of the road. When he hung up, he told me his guy was going to pull up in ten minutes. I handed him a stack of money, and he counted it in front of me, twice. Flip put the money in his pocket. A car pulled up and parked in front of my Lexus. Flip got out, and then he got into the passenger side of the other car.

I sat in my car with my hand on my handgun. It seemed like forever passed as I ran through all the possible scenarios I was facing. The passenger side window of the other car rolled down. Flip stuck his arm out the window and motioned me to follow them. The car in front of me crept down the road until it was around the corner in the subdivision. Then the car stopped in the middle of the road. I stopped my Lexus behind it.

Flip got out of the passenger seat and walked back to my car. He got in my car, and he told me there was a problem. I frowned as I asked what was going on.

"There's four hundred dollars missing. You didn't give me enough money."

"Dude, you counted it in front of me twice."

"I must have counted wrong. I need more."

"I gave you the right amount. We both counted it. I gave you all of it."

"Hang on…"

Flip jumped out of my car and jogged back to the car in the middle of the road in front of my new Lexus. Another two minutes passed, and he stepped back out of the other car. As Flip walked back to me, the car in front of me peeled out and drove away. Flip got back in my car. He tossed me a sealed freezer bag, pulled from under his shirt. It looked like the proper amount, and I began driving out of the subdivision.

Flip kept insisting I owed him another four hundred dollars. I kept insisting that he was trying to run a con on me. We made it back across the city to Flip's house, and I parked around the corner. I told Flip to search the car underneath his seat, and on the floor, to see if he dropped the money. I watched as he acted like he was looking for money. He happened to pull my gun holster from the floor behind the seat. His demeanor changed.

"What's this?"

"The holster for my gun."

"Where's the gun?"

"In my pocket."

"Uh…I'm not afraid of guns. I…uh…you should have told me you had a gun with you. I wouldn't have brought the cleaver."

Flip ran his mouth a bit when we were back inside his apartment. He insisted I shorted him on the money. I sucked up my pride, and I threw a quarter ounce down onto a plate to appease Flip's incessant complaining. I told Melanie we were leaving. I was mad throughout the entire drive back to Melanie's house. I didn't give her any money for her trouble that night. Instead, I scooped the shake from the bottom of the bag, and I left her with what I was fairly sure was garbage someone had added to make the weight I had purchased.

I left Dayton in a bad mood despite buying a new car that day. I drove the Lexus back to my storage unit in Perrysburg. I decided to sleep in my car at the storage unit that night. When I woke up the next morning, I had a thought. I inspected the underside of the passenger seat of my new car. To my half-surprise, I found four hundred dollars underneath the seat in my Lexus. Melanie either reconsidered, or she just couldn't locate the cash which Flip had tried to remove from my possession the night before.

...

Buying the Lexus meant I had yet another car which needed an audio upgrade. The Lexus had a premium sound system already. There were eleven speakers and an amplifier. I had four amplifiers and another twenty speakers to add to the system. I also spent seven hundred dollars to order a top-of-the-line interface to run with the control computer of the car. Dan and I had much more work to do at Dan's house in Lansing.

The days and nights of partying at Dan's house continued. While my BMW sat in the back yard, I used my Lexus to travel as I pleased. My interactions with people from the website and the phone apps remained in full swing. My drug consumption never ceased. Dan, same as my friend Kevin, liked being the big man in the drug scene. I managed to remain a ghost to all but my closest friends in Lansing.

The scene there in Lansing seemed far more treacherous than the scene in Detroit. Everyone knew each other. The groups and alliances all seemed precarious. People backstabbed people they said were friends. Mostly everyone chased influence and wished to be top dog in the Lansing underworld scene. I wanted nothing to do with notoriety. I was there to work on my car. I was fine with Dan soaking up the attention.

One night, I returned from a visit to a friend. As I passed

through Ann Arbor during a snowstorm, I hit a patch of black ice on an interstate overpass. My car spun as it slid into a cement barricade at the top of the overpass. I smashed my bumper and front end of my Lexus into the concrete as I slid across the bridge. My car was still running, so I continued the drive through the storm back to Dan's house.

The next day, I ordered twenty-two parts so Dan would be able to fix my car. I spent two weeks stuck at his house again. Though the parts all arrived within two days of ordering them, Dan seemed to drag out the repairs. He was doing as he had done with the BMW.

Dan liked having me there to provide drugs and order food every single day. Dan came and went as he pleased. I had people over on occasion for sexual intimacy. Sometimes, I would get picked up to go hang out at other houses. Mostly though, I had to pester Dan to work on my car to get it back in running condition. For the time, it sat alongside my inoperable BMW out in the yard.

After what seemed like forever, my Lexus was finally back to running condition. I needed to take trips to see people all over. I crisscrossed the Midwest and stacked money once again. I also continued to add to my video collection of shared intimate moments with sexual partners.

I stayed in hotel rooms around Michigan in all the major cities. Online interactions became real-world dynamics. If friends from around the country were anywhere close to me, we would get a hotel room and explore intimacy together anytime we could. Some interactions were a long time coming. Others were impulsive meetings.

I drove west late one night to meet a woman at a diner for coffee. We met and talked, but the connection just wasn't there. When the woman left, I walked out to my car and began checking the apps on my phone. I was in Grand Rapids, and I figured I would find someone close to meet with me before I drove back to Lansing.

I came across a stunningly beautiful trans girl on one of

the dating apps. I sent her a message. Selena was interested right away.

"I'm at a hotel with my ex. Come here. I'd love to see you."

"Na, I'm not trying to meet up with multiple people."

Selena had gone out to dinner with her ex, who was in town from New York. She had been hanging out with him at his hotel because she had no other plans for the night. I pulled into the hotel. I saw Selena walk into one of the rooms across the parking lot. She saw me, and she held up a finger to let me know she would be a minute. I waited. A text came through.

"Okay, I'm leaving now. Follow me."

I had on a baseball cap and an unflattering poofy winter coat. When I stepped from my car to walk up to Selena's apartment with her, I noticed the way she looked at me. We walked up the flights of stairs and into the apartment. She was still looking at me with suspicion. I played into it. I could tell Selena thought I was catfishing her. She stood there in her living room, looking standoffish. I smiled.

"Am I not what you expected? How about I fix that for you."

I took off my poofy coat and my baseball hat. Selena breathed a sigh of relief. She walked up to me and wrapped her arms around me. She had legitimately thought I was a catfish. She thought the pictures on my profile were of someone else. Once I took off my outerwear, Selena saw I was exactly who I portrayed on the internet.

"My profile pictures are from this week."

"I believe you. I just hadn't been sure when you were all covered up."

Selena and I did crystal, and we made love all over Selena's living room. I filled her as we switched positions in different places on the floor. We kissed passionately on the couch. We stretched our intimacy well into early the next afternoon. We both reached a point of sweaty exhaustion.

I ordered a pizza from an app on my phone. Figuring they would leave the food at the door, Selena and I took a shower together. Twenty minutes into our make-out session, as the shower water cascaded over us, the bathroom door suddenly opened. I was in shock. The pizza delivery guy had not only walked into the apartment after nobody answered the door, but he even walked into the bathroom while we were showering.

I grabbed a towel and chased the guy out of the apartment. I was mad about the invasion of privacy, but I also had another concern. Selena and I had been in the shower in the bathroom. The pizza guy had to walk through the living room to reach the bathroom. I had a handgun, drugs, and paraphernalia strewn about openly on the couch. I evaluated my belongings. Nothing had been taken, but it would have been impossible to walk by the couch without at least seeing the interesting items sitting there.

Selena and I took a nap after we ate the pizza. When we woke up, it was dark in Selena's bedroom.

"I'm going out to eat with some friends of mine. You can come, if you want to."

"I can't. I have to stop back in Lansing and see a few people before I head out of town again. My phone's blowing up right now."

Sirius

The 2019/2020 winter was wearing on me mentally. The drama in Lansing was continuous. I did my best to avoid it, but just being where I was, it brought the drama to me. I wanted out. Lex had helped me buy a car; she invited me to use that car to come stay in Manhattan. I liked the idea, and I made the necessary trip to my storage unit to grab the belongings I wanted with me in New York City.

Though Elaine had asked me to leave her house in Upstate New York months earlier, she had later apologized. We had been back in contact with one another, and Elaine wished to see me again. I had other friends in Upstate New York I wished to see as well. Before I drove to Manhattan to stay with Lex, I stayed in Poughkeepsie again for a short while.

One afternoon, I was alone at Elaine's house while she was at work. She texted and told me that she looked forward to intimacy with me once she returned home. I decided to take a shower and make some videos. I figured the best way to create any sort of video content was to set up the camera outside the bathtub and just let it record the entire time I was in the shower.

At some point in the shower, I decided to shave. I lifted the razor up to the showerhead to rinse it out. I lowered my hand with the razor from up by the showerhead. My hand dropped down to my side. As it did, I felt a sudden sharp pain in a sensitive location.

My mouth dropped open as my eyes suddenly widened. I looked down as I grabbed myself by the base. Blood was pouring from me. I had cut the end of myself from the hole to the bottom of the head. I looked at my phone, still recording video, and I laughed when I realized I had the incident on video. I stayed in the shower and poured blood for the next half hour. I wrapped myself in gauze and sent the video to Elaine.

"I don't think intimacy is going to be possible tonight. I'm sorry."

After multiple stops to visit friends, I drove around to take the George Washington Bridge to enter Manhattan from New Jersey. I paid the sixteen-dollar toll, and I crossed the bridge. The traffic on the FDR was bumper to bumper, but cars were moving at a fast pace. Ambulances and police cruisers with sirens and flashing lights were all over the freeway, stuck in the traffic the same as every other vehicle. Nobody moved over for them. There were never any open lanes into which to move.

After I thrice circled the block on the corner of 23rd Street and the FDR in midtown Manhattan, I finally found a parking space. Lex came down and helped me with some of my bags. She used her keycard to open the door to her apartment building. Once I had everything in Lex's apartment, the two of us had sex for the first time in our lives. Lex went to bed afterward. I stayed awake to record the sunrise over the East River from the eighth-floor apartment.

Lex worked on the weekdays. She also went to work from her company's Texas office every other week for long weekends. I had a lot of time to myself. I walked to meet people from the internet in midtown Manhattan. I preferred to walk because it was hard to find a parking space in the city.

There was a parking garage close to Lex's apartment complex. It would have cost me hundreds of dollars a month to put my car in a garage. Any of the metered spaces on the streets would have cost far more than the parking garages. Instead, I chose to follow the rules of the street signs.

If I was fortunate enough to find a spot on the service drive on 23rd Street, I had to be sure I knew how long I was able to park. The signs in the streets were confusing. Days, hours, special situations, all were indicated on the signs. Signs posted with other signs superseded even more signs. Some days, loading zones were a factor. Some days, street cleaning was a factor.

Most mornings required at least two moves of my car. I would go downstairs and walk to wherever my car was parked. If I didn't choose to remain in my car, I would have to find another parking space before I could go back inside. If I chose to wait in my car for events such as street cleaning, I would pull out of the space when the street sweeper was a couple spaces behind me and try to race around the block to get back to the space before some other car parked in it.

I was barely ever lucky enough to drive around the block and still have my parking space available. Often, it would be a car I drove behind, one which had pulled out of a space in front of me, who ended up taking my spot when we both reached the original side of the building. The stress from trying to find a parking spot anywhere in midtown Manhattan was enough to make me walk to any destination within a ten-block radius of the apartment complex.

I walked outside one evening to drive somewhere. I had parking tickets underneath my windshield wiper. I got a ticket for not having a front license plate. Though my back plate was an out-of-state Ohio license plate, New York City hit me with the infraction. I also had a ticket for the clear license plate cover which I had transferred from the BMW to the back of my Lexus. It was absolutely clear, yet I was hit with obstructing visibility of my back license plate.

On the days Lex worked, she ordered food when she came home in the evenings. Lex and I walked around midtown Manhattan after we ate our food. She took me to markets and cafes. She showed me around her hundred and eighty-five-building apartment community. The buildings had their own library, a park, and even an ice-skating rink during the winter months.

Lex took me to the building which housed the head office

of the apartment community. A lady working behind the desk took my picture. The lady had me fill out some paperwork with my personal information. I was given a photo-ID and a keycard showing I was a resident of the apartment community. I no longer needed to be buzzed in when I went out to move my car to other parking spaces. I didn't need anyone to operate the intercoms or the elevators after that. I was able to come and go as I pleased.

For reasons unknown to me, one of the dating apps on my phone locked me out of my profile. Instead of attempting to get back into the old profile, I created a new profile at noon one day in Manhattan. I then forgot about it until the evening. I checked the app at five o'clock that same day. I had seventy messages from women in Manhattan who wished to meet me. Seventy messages in the five hours since I had made my new profile…

I spent the next week being taken out to dinner at fancy restaurants in various parts of the city. The women were doctors, fashion designers, business owners, television news personalities, and wealthy entrepreneurs. I enjoyed the fine dining experiences, but I knew I didn't fit in with that part of society. I never slept with any of the ladies. I did share a sweet and memorable kiss on the sidewalk with one of those women after we finished eating dinner at an exclusive restaurant in Greenwich Village.

I agreed to meet the woman for dinner one evening. I was on a return trip from New Jersey that particular day. The restaurant was conveniently located close to where I just returned to Manhattan through the Holland Tunnel. I even managed to find a decent parking spot close to the restaurant with minimal effort. That evening in Greenwich Village had gone better than my time earlier that day in Newark, New Jersey.

The day prior, I began interacting with an Asian transgender girl on a different app on my phone. We video-called that night. She invited me to her house in Newark. We agreed on a time that next morning for me to see her. The girl was twenty-four, and she still lived with her family.

"I have total privacy, though. The back part was converted to my own apartment."

I took the Holland Tunnel into New Jersey. I pulled up to Mika's house right on time, eleven o'clock in the morning. Mika walked out from the back of her house and into my car. Mika and I drove around for a while as we talked and decided where we wanted to eat. We found a little college-like area with a movie theatre and rows of restaurants on each side of the street. Once we finished eating lunch, we headed back to Mika's house.

Mika and I spent the next four hours naked in her bed. We made love, rested, cuddled, and made love some more. During our intimacy, I took a minute to order food from an app on my phone. We both had worked up another appetite. Time went by, and the two of us continued to interact unclothed in Mika's bedroom apartment at the back of her house.

Eventually, my hunger and curiosity got the best of me. The food should have been to us long ago. It wasn't. The app indicated that the food had been delivered. I had specified that the delivery driver needed to knock on the door at the back of the house. I doubted we had missed the knock. Though we were enjoying each other in the bed, the door was only feet from where we were being intimate. I spent the next half hour on the phone with customer service.

"Sir, it's up to the driver how they proceed if nobody answers the door."

"Nobody even ever knocked…"

"That doesn't matter."

"What? What happened to the food?"

"Sir, I don't have an answer for you."

They didn't offer any resolution. Eventually, I gave up. It was getting late. I had a date in Greenwich Village I didn't want to miss.

Before I came to Manhattan, I had ordered my first tattoo kit. The kit came to Dan's house in Lansing while I was staying there. I tattooed myself for the first time before I drove out to New York. It was during my days in that eighth-floor apartment in Manhattan when I began to cover my left arm in ink. Manhattan was where I started the process, a process which became normal for me as I traveled. Though Lex had no tattoos and didn't want me to tattoo her, my practice on myself became my first step to tattooing many other people.

Lex didn't do crystal, so I did hotrails by myself while I was in Manhattan...unless I happened to visit someone who was also into partying. The entire time I was away from the Midwest, I was constantly receiving messages from people wanting me to come back to party. A friend of mine who lived in Ann Arbor sent me a message. That message made me realize I needed to return so I could stack money again. The amount I knew I was going to make was enough for me to return to the Midwest.

On the day I left Manhattan, I had one more stop in the area to make. A Greek transgender girl in her twenties had been interacting with me for about a week. I told her I was going to stop and see her on my way out of the city. I crossed the Williamsburg Bridge to Queens and spent the afternoon with her. As I dropped her off and prepared to leave New York, my phone finally completely broke as a result of falling in Cedar Falls at Hocking Hills almost a year earlier.

I was fed up with electronics in general. I drove back across the bridge to Manhattan, and I drove across the George Washington bridge into New Jersey. It was nighttime as I crossed the state. When I reached the Delaware Water Gap, I barely had time to grab an older phone to record video while I drove past a forest fire on the side of a mountain. My old phone had a battery issue which caused it to lose all of its charge within ten minutes, but that was enough time for me to record the forest fire around me. I posted the video, then the phone died.

I stopped at a rest stop when I got tired of driving; I was between Pittsburgh and Cleveland. I managed to drive from New York City to the Midwest without GPS. I put the shades in my car's windows, and I spent a few hours videoing back and forth with a girl from Brooklyn while my old phone remained charging on a battery pack as I used it.

The next morning, I continued to Michigan. By late afternoon, it was raining while I was on I-96 approaching Lansing. Dan was hanging out at an apartment which two of our friends rented. Simon and Caleb had been dating since autumn of 2019. They moved in together around the same time they began dating. Simon was Black, Caleb was White. Simon was tall, Caleb was not. Simon was an aspiring hip-hop dancer and singer, Caleb was ex-military. Simon had never been with a woman, Caleb had never been with a man...until he met Simon. Simon did drugs...Caleb did drugs.

I texted Dan to let him know I was on the interstate, ten minutes from the apartment. I quickly turned off my old phone so it would still have a little bit of charge. The rain had intensified. I was driving seventy miles an hour, despite the rain. Had I known I had worn the tread off of my tires from all my travel, I most likely would have been a bit more careful in the rain. Suddenly, my car began to hydroplane on the wet road.

Before I knew it, I spun halfway around, and I was sliding down the interstate backward. I could see the looks of shock on the faces of the couple in the car behind me. I was facing them as they were driving forward. I was traveling at almost seventy miles an hour...backward.

My car drifted towards the median which separated the two directions of traffic. My Lexus cut a quarter mile of muddy tracks into the median as I hydroplaned off the road and into the grass. At one point, my car lifted onto two wheels. I hoped to not flip over. Beside me in the driver's seat, my car was packed full of heavy bags and other items I had failed to drop off at my storage unit.

As I began to slow, the right side of my car lowered, and all four wheels slid along the ground again. I was still sliding backwards toward the ditch in the center of the median, but at least I wasn't upside down. It was the ditch itself which finally stopped my car. I was facing the wrong way, and the water of the ditch came up to the bottom of my car doors.

I pushed my door down into the water and climbed out of my car. That couple in the car that was behind me stopped their car on the shoulder.

"Are you alright?"

"I'm good. Can you call the police for me? You don't need to wait around."

Besides being submerged to the bottom of the car doors in a ditch, a ditch which was slowly rising as the rain continued to fall, I only noticed one part of my car which was damaged. The bumper I replaced just prior to heading to New York was ripped from my car. I found half of it a hundred yards from my car's resting place in the ditch. It was shredded. I left it there. My concern soon switched to the rising water. Two police cruisers arrived.

"You're alright? Can I see your insurance information?"

"Sure. Give me just a minute."

I ran back down into the median through the wet grass and weeds. I climbed back in my car and turned on my phone with the short-lasting battery. I pulled up my insurance website, and I entered my information. My policy had expired. I sat for another five minutes, praying that my phone didn't die on me as I renewed my policy while the water level rose higher around my car.

I ran, with my dying phone, back up the wet grass to the police cruisers on the shoulder of the highway. I handed an officer my phone to record my insurance information.

"Can I have that back as soon as possible? The battery's gonna die. Can you call me a tow truck?"

As soon as my phone was handed back to me, I texted Dan my location and shut it off.

"A tow truck is on the way."

"Thank you. I'm headed back to my car. The water's rising. I need to get some stuff moved around, quick."

I managed to fill my seats with my belongings at the same

time the water began to flow into the car from the driver's side, the side which was angled downward into the middle of the ditch. I grabbed my laptop bag and my backpack full of drugs. I shut the door to the car. I went back up to the road where the police were sitting.

When the wrecker showed up, I helped the tow truck driver hook the chains to my car. The wrecker pulled my Lexus up to the road in front of the police cruisers. I turned my phone on for a minute to see if Dan replied. I had texted him my location so he would come to help me out. I had a text message reply. Dan told me he had driven by, but he didn't stop when he saw the police were there with me. I turned my phone off again.

The driver of the tow truck asked me where I wanted my car towed. I thought for a second. I had an idea. My car was caked in mud and grass. I had no front bumper...again. Unlike the time before, when I had hit the cement barricade on the overpass in Ann Arbor, I did still have both headlights. I told the tow truck driver to hold on while I talked to the officers.

"Guys, I have an idea. Instead of being towed somewhere, I just want to drive the car if I can get it to start."

"We don't see an issue with that."

"I'm good then?"

"Technically, we could site you for traveling at unsafe speeds in relation to the road conditions, but the evening you're having already seems rough. Go ahead."

"Alright guys, thanks for the help."

I stepped back into my mud-covered car and prayed to myself again. I prayed that the bumper was the only thing broken on my car. I tried to start the engine...and it started on the first try. I put my car in drive, and I took off. One more time, I powered up my phone. Dan called me seconds later.

"I'm up and running."

"Where do you want me to meet you?"

We met in a parking lot at the next exit from the interstate. Dan then followed me back to his house. Later that night, Dan took me back to where I hydroplaned and spun into the median. We walked the trail of mud and tire tracks which my car had created earlier that night. We found the other half of my bumper. I left it there. Dan took me back to his house. I once again had to order parts for my Lexus. I decided to upgrade, and I ordered a nine-hundred-dollar custom Lexus bumper with the newer wide-mouth grill. It was the bumper I always wished was on the car anyhow.

All Quiet on the Western Front

March of 2020 had an ominous feel to it. Whisperings of a crisis reached even those like me who watched no television at all. I had my new custom bumper on my Lexus. My car was ready to travel. Three weeks into March, the governor of Michigan declared a lockdown for everyone in the state. That same afternoon, I left for Texas.

I had been texting and interacting with a transgender girl in her mid-twenties from a dating app on my phone. She lived in Austin, Texas. I had never been to Texas, but I was in the process of traveling to all of the states I hadn't yet visited. Maria invited me to stay with her in Austin. Maria didn't think anything of the invitation, until I told her I was on my way.

I sat at Simon and Caleb's apartment as five people who never watched television were all glued to the tv screen. It was late afternoon. I had just made a couple trips in the Lansing area. I was ready to relax, until the news report confirmed what all of us were waiting to see. At midnight that night, Michigan was going to go on lockdown. I packed up my paraphernalia and yelled for last call.

"Everybody, get what you need now. I'm about to disappear for a while."

The surface streets of Lansing, Michigan were empty when I pulled from the apartment complex. The city was a ghost town that evening. I had an electric tingling feeling as I made my way to the interstate. I had never seen a rush hour in a city as vacant as was the rush hour that day. I felt an odd connection to the world around me. The population of the state was acting as one. The government managed to get their point across. The streets were silent.

It was a surreal drive to my storage unit in Ohio. There were a few cars on the roads, but I mostly saw cargo trucks. Police, which normally sat in medians to catch speeders, were absent from their posts. I reached my storage unit in Ohio much faster than usual. There was minimal traffic in the Toledo area as well.

I drove for two days, stopping at rest stops along the way. Hotrails fueled my travel. Hotrails fueled my rest. I entered Texas for the first time in my life on a hot and humid afternoon. I pulled off the road to a rest stop so I could update Maria and respond to the messages from everyone else. Police cruisers patrolled the rest stop in Texas. My hotrail consumption was not affected in any way.

It was the middle of the night when I reached Austin, Texas. I parked my car in the parking lot of the apartment building, and I put the shades up in all the windows. I grabbed my bags of belongings, and I headed up the stairs outside the apartment units.

Maria was happy to join me in blowing down hotrails once I settled in. I was normally the person who talked the most. Maria took that position from the very beginning. I wasn't sure if the crystal was the cause of her abstract thought processes, but I was fairly certain the drugs exacerbated any underlying condition Maria may have had. She was full of thoughts for which I had no response.

"A secret society has a hit out on me… I've already defended myself against multiple assassination attempts… My father was a disgraced member of a national militant minority group…"

Maria believed famous rappers had hidden messages in their music, deliberately placed there to warn her of attempts on her life. She believed she was meant to rise to power, but she always needed to be on alert for those wishing to keep her from her destiny.

I listened to Maria's thoughts. I had no insights to add to

what she told me. I welcomed her hands when she put them on my body. I was far more comfortable with sexual intimacy than trying to absorb Maria's grandiose delusions. The two hours the two of us spent being sexual that first night was an enjoyable distraction from my own mind, wondering what I got myself into.

I had a different friend from a dating app who lived in a suburb of Austin. I had already let her know I was coming to the Austin area. After I woke up the next morning at Maria's apartment, I let Beth know I was available to visit her. Beth sent me her address, and I took a forty-five-minute drive from the middle of Austin to a suburb northeast of the city.

I parked on the street in front of Beth's house. Her neighborhood was upper-middle class. Large homes, manicured lawns, and swimming pools filled the subdivision. Kids played in the yards. Sedans and SUVs were parked on the cement driveways. Beth met me at her door. We hugged, and she invited me in.

I talked with Beth as we sat on couches in her living room. Suddenly, I opened my eyes; four hours had passed. I had fallen asleep sitting up on Beth's black leather couch. I woke up in the same position. I thanked my friend for letting me sleep. I was slightly embarrassed. Two of Beth's younger children asked me if I had a good nap.

Later that evening, after exploring the city of Austin by myself, I drove back to Maria's apartment. A few minutes after I was back inside, I went to use the bathroom. As I sat on the toilet, the door to the bathroom kicked open. Before I could say a word, I was being accused of being part of a secret assassination plot. I finished in the bathroom, but the accusations and yelling continued. I gathered my belongings, and I left the apartment. I had no idea what had just happened, but I knew my time with Maria was finished.

I left Austin that night. I decided to travel to Houston. I drove on into the night as crystal fueled me. I reached the Houston area on an interstate. I traversed what I thought was the main metro area of the city. I was preparing to continue to drive east, and then I came up to downtown Houston. I spent the next two hours recording video as I crisscrossed the highway interchanges downtown.

I left Houston after I recorded enough video. I headed to the Gulf Coast. When I reached Galveston, the roads were as empty as they had been when I left Lansing. Even in the early hours of morning, I was surprised at how few cars were on the streets. I decided to rest in my Lexus in Galveston that morning. When the sun rose, I bought food from a drive-thru restaurant. The videos I took of the empty city were hauntingly beautiful. The ominous vibe I felt that night in Galveston, Texas had me feeling that it was just the beginning of a changing time...with ramifications I was yet to experience.

I drove along the coast on the interstate through Texas. The next morning, I continued on to Louisiana. I reached New Orleans the next evening. There was traffic, but the pandemic resulted in a strange feel to my travel. Weekday traffic was as sparse as a Sunday. Semitrucks dominated the roadways. Downtown New Orleans had minimal congestion. I recorded more videos as I drove through the city at night.

I made the mistake of letting my gas tank run almost empty before I reached the Lake Pontchartrain Causeway as I left New Orleans. I reached Mandeville on the north side of the lake as fumes carried me to the closest gas station. It was a huge relief when I filled up my gas tank. I was surprised I made it across the lake. I expected to be stranded somewhere on the middle of the bridge.

I drove through Mississippi and into Alabama. I stopped to rest at an Alabama rest stop. At sunrise the next morning, I continued east. I was on my way to Florida. I wanted to see Sarah again in Kissimmee. I let her know I was coming to see her. I didn't think she believed I was serious.

No Time is a Good Time

Sarah was in the side yard of her house when I pulled up. She saw me as I walked up to her. It wasn't until I was in front of her that I saw recognition in her eyes. Even then, Sarah didn't seem happy to see me. I only received a hug when I asked her for one. Sarah insisted she had to go back inside before her mom knew she was in the yard. I walked back to my car, feeling dejected.

I responded to a message on an app as I was leaving Sarah's subdivision. Ivan was in his early twenties. He had bleached-blonde hair and an athletic build. He was from eastern Europe, but he had a house in Kissimmee while he went to college in America. Ivan invited me over. It was a five-minute drive from Sarah's house to his.

The next morning, I told Sarah I still wanted to see her before I left the area. She told me to meet her at the gas station in front of her subdivision. I waited for her in my car. When Sarah walked up and got in, she had me drive her to a park on a small lake across the highway from the gas station.

Sarah showed me around the park. We walked out on the docks. We wandered around. We talked as we looked out across the water. Once we left the park, I drove down the main strip in Kissimmee and into some random neighborhoods. We continued to talk.

"I need to get back home. My mom…"

"Alright, I'm gonna get a hotel room tonight. I want to see you more."

"I'll do all I can to get away. I can't promise anything…"

I managed to find a hotel room right next to Disney World

with the travel app on my phone. Whether it was a pandemic discount, or not, the total cost ended up at seventeen dollars. Sarah never spent any more time with me that night. She claimed her mom wouldn't let her leave. I stayed in the hotel room by myself that evening. As I walked to a soda machine in the middle of the night, the hotel door caught the curtain in the window. The door was stuck closed with me outside the room. It took a half hour before a maintenance worker was able to let me back in the room.

I stayed around the Orlando area for one more day after I left the hotel the next morning. The people who were active outside were still going about their daily routines…there were just fewer of them. When the sun went down that night, I met up with a woman from one of the dating apps. We met at a park playground. I pushed her on a swing in the dark as we talked about ourselves and about the panic that was steadily overtaking the entire country. After we parted ways, I drove north to leave Florida.

I was in Georgia eating a burrito in my car the next afternoon when police surrounded me. Five cruisers pulled up to me from all directions. I continued to eat as I rolled down the window.

"We received a call of someone sitting in a car, possibly casing the area."

"Yeah, I'm sure I'm the guy." I took another bite of my burrito. "I just needed to eat and rest. I'm headed back to Michigan from Florida. Long drive."

"Well, yeah. That's a long way to go. Stay safe, sir. Sorry to bother you." The police left me alone to finish my meal.

Ziah and I had been texting back and forth during that trip down South. I was all over the place. Ziah was locked down with her mom and her mom's girlfriend in Surf City, North Carolina. I video-called with her from parking lots and rest stops. We talked about seeing each other again.

"I want to see you again. I'm gonna come see you."

"You can try. I'm not sure I'm going to be able to leave here."

"Well, I'm gonna try. It's worth it to me to give it a shot."

...

I was in the mountains of Tennessee when Dan sent me a strange text. I pulled into a gas station, and I made a phone call.

"There's a lot I can't say on the phone, but everything in Lansing is all messed up."

"What do you mean? Are you in danger?"

"No, I'm not. I can't say too much. I'll see you sometime soon, I hope."

"Alright, man. Be safe."

I factored the interaction to tweaking, but I was left with some concerns when I hung up the phone. I pulled from the gas station to continue my drive.

...

Surf City was its own island off the coast of North Carolina. There was a bridge from the mainland to the island, full of beach homes and summer homes. I arrived on the island at eleven o'clock at night. Ziah apologized to me. Her mom wasn't allowing her to leave to see anyone. I drove around while on the island. I missed Ziah, and I was sad I wasn't able to see her that night.

Soon, my focus turned to how I was the absolute only car on the streets of the island. I didn't see a single person as I drove around. I didn't see a single car on the road. Not just was there nobody else driving on the roads, there was nobody even parked on any of the streets anywhere.

I was tired from driving. Hotrails couldn't overcome my desire to shut my eyes. I drove through the dark streets of Surf City as I looked for inconspicuous parking. I turned a corner into one of the neighborhoods, and I decided it was as good of a place as any to put the shades up in my windows and get some sleep.

At four in the morning, I woke up to tapping on my windshield. I opened my eyes in the darkness and sat there in silence for a few seconds. There was a louder noise on my windshield. I yelled for them to hold on a second. I didn't want my windshield to break. I made sure my hotrail equipment was put away, and I opened my car door.

"I just needed to rest. I've been driving all day..."

Both of the officers were shocked that I drove from Florida and was still in the process of driving to the Midwest. The officers offered up some close locations with parking spots. I thanked them. They apologized for waking me and wished me safe travels. The interaction was my prompt to leave the island. I blew down a hotrail as I crossed the bridge back to the mainland. I texted Ziah. I told her I was leaving the area.

I found a rest stop outside Wilmington, and I slept until it was light outside the next morning. I sent a message to a lady from the website. She was down in Southern Georgia. I told her I would be happy to see her in the next few days. I began another drive south.

...

I had been in contact with another woman from Kentucky. She had invited me to come to see her, but she wasn't intimidated by the global crisis. She wanted me to come stay with her at her house. I told her I was on my way.

When I reached the Louisville area, I put my phone in the holder on my windshield. I saw the city skyline through the trees, and I pressed the button to record video as I drove. The Louisville sky that evening was a dark blue. I headed south on the interstate. The sun was setting over the rivers and bridges on the right side of the highway. There were four lanes for each direction on the interstate. The downtown Louisville skyline was approaching on my left. It was rush-hour on a weekday. I knew I had stumbled into another one of those moments which was larger than I.

The back of my neck tingled as I suddenly cleared the tree line on both sides of the highway. The space in front of me opened up to a concrete jungle of overpasses and underpasses. The river paralleled the highway to the right of my car. Bridges of varied sizes and shapes crossed over the expanse above the water. The lights from the skyscrapers shone from the downtown area on my left. Besides just a handful of other drivers, I was alone.

A major city at rush hour on one side of me and a sunset over the river on the other side...and almost nobody else anywhere around me sharing the experience. It was surreal, to say the least. My eyes watered. It was beautifully haunting beyond words. The video I recorded that evening was forty minutes long. It spanned from Kentucky to Illinois and back to Kentucky again. It crossed the river and the state lines. It began with a dark blue sky and ended in the night.

Those first two minutes as I drove past downtown Louisville became one of the most amazing videos I ever created. I almost missed recording it; I had seen the tops of the skyscrapers for only a split-second as I approached. I made a fateful decision in that moment. I began recording, and I managed to record a magical moment in my life.

I stopped for gas a half hour from Devon's house. I did a double take when I saw the sign displaying the cost-per-gallon of gasoline. Frowning, I confirmed the price on the sign with the digital display on the gas pump. It was legit, and it was the first time I had seen that price for gas in two decades. Gas at that gas station was ninety-nine cents a gallon.

Devon instructed me where to park in her yard. She owned a lot of property in the rolling farmland hills of deep Kentucky. I parked next to the barn. Once inside, Devon and I quickly headed to the bedroom. We kissed and embraced. We undressed as we made our way to the bed. The crystal affected me that evening. What I couldn't do with intercourse I made up for with my mouth. After Devon climaxed, she went to sleep.

Devon had the next day off work. She rode with me and showed me around the local area. We went out to eat, we went to the store, and we went to the post office. Devon needed to mail some letters. I was happy to see the city. Later that evening, we cooked dinner together.

Devon worked normal business hours on the five weekdays. I split my time on those days. Half of the time, I did hotrails at the dining room table. I spent the rest of the time making erotic art videos. I made videos fully naked in the front yard...until I saw three older cowboy-looking characters seated out front of the house across the street. Devon's front yard was a large field with a pond, and her house was offset fairly far from the road. The house across the street was set the same way, but it was a clear view from one front porch to the other.

I received a text message one afternoon from Dan's friend Tammy in Lansing. The text wasn't like any of the messages she usually sent me. It was blatantly urgent.

"Dan disappeared. The house is gone. So is your BMW."

I called Tammy. She answered right away.

"What are you talking about?"

"Something happened. A guy came in with a gun. Police are looking for Dan and Ashley. There's a news story. It's all messed up. Everything's gone. More is gonna happen." Tammy was all over the place.

I told Devon I had to leave Kentucky. I continued to try to call Dan, but I only ever reached his voicemail. I sent messages to some of our other friends in Lansing. They knew something was going on, but they didn't know the details.

I texted my friend Brittany to see if she knew anything. Brittany and her best friend Ashley spent a lot of time over at Dan's house when I was around. Brittany sent me a link to a news story. It didn't answer my questions, but it did show me something. The news clip was short. I knew the people in the video.

The scene up in Lansing was in a downward spiral. Though I avoided the drama, I could feel the tension prior to my departure to Texas. The sinister undertones in Lansing were the catalyst to leave the area for a while. The lock down was the final push to head out. The text from Tammy pulled me back in. I couldn't shake a feeling; if I didn't wrap up Lansing's loose ends in a timely manner, I wouldn't be able to leave.

We Are the Company We Keep

I reached Lansing in the afternoon. The sky was gray. Mindset matched the dreary weather. Clouds shrouded the city, a metaphorical manifestation of my mental state. I felt a storm approaching.

People were walking all around outside the shopping center. Tammy was standing on the pavement, at the curb by the traffic lane. She was looking for me. I muted the stereo as I pulled up. I pushed the button to unlock the door. She slid into my car.

Tammy and I matched gazes. I sensed the turmoil in her thoughts. She didn't have the luxury to leave the city whenever she felt like it. I felt a twinge of sympathy for her as I saw the desperation in her eyes. Her demeanor added to the gray and overcast day. I tried to remain positive. Something caught my attention. Tammy's right hand was wrapped up in bandages.

"What happened?"

As she began to tell a story, Tammy unwrapped the bandages from her hand. I looked over to a horrific sight; her hand was shredded and mangled. I saw the layers of meat down to the bones. I saw tendons, ligaments, and all the intricate details of the insides of a human hand, details that should never be exposed. I was aghast. With my eyes open wide, I asked Tammy if she needed medical attention.

"I'll take you to the hospital right now..."

"No. I'm not going to the hospital."

Tammy rewrapped her hand with the bandages. My eyes remained open wide. My mouth had dropped open as well. I decided not to push the issue. I wasn't sure why she refused medical treatment, but I decided it wasn't my business.

Tammy first wanted me to drive her to a shady apartment complex, only a half mile from Dan's recently vacated house. I remained in my car as she ran inside to pick up whatever it was she wanted to pick up. I would later read about an incident at those apartments, taking place only months later. Those apartments; where Tammy used a butcher's knife to stab a guy in the heart, killing him on his balcony…allegedly.

Tammy and I pulled from the parking lot to the surface streets. I had prepared the hotrail tray while she was inside the apartment. I blew down a large line of crystal and passed the tray. Tammy stopped about halfway through her line. She looked at me.

"That's so much. It's too much. I can't…"

"You have to. I wanna do more. I'm ready to dump more on the tray."

Tammy and I spent the rest of the afternoon driving up and down the streets of Lansing, Michigan. I drove and prepared the drugs, Tammy did her thing on her phone. As the light in the sky began to fade, she received confirmation of Dan's location. She gave me an address. I typed the address into my GPS. I was ten minutes from Dan's location.

"I'm gonna make a quick stop."

I went inside the rest stop to use the bathroom and the vending machine. I came back out to my car. I cracked my windows as the two of us filled the car with meth smoke. My hand twitched as I broke up another eightball. All the crystal from the tray dumped all over the floor of my car, coating my feet in powder. Deciding it was a lost cause, I dropped another eightball of crystal on the tray. The two of us each blew down a hotrail line. I then pulled from the rest stop, back on track to find Dan. I was six minutes away, according to GPS. It was late evening, and it was dark outside.

Tammy's mangled hand had resulted from an incident at Dan's house earlier in the week. According to her, that incident caused the rift between her, and Dan. I pulled into the complex of town houses. To avoid potential violence, Tammy advised me to leave her on the opposite side of the complex. I stopped my car and let her out. She assured me someone was on the way to pick her up. I thanked her for the help, and I drove alone to the other side of the neighborhood of townhouses.

I found the specific address, and I parked my car in the driveway. I grabbed my backpack, and I tapped underneath my shirt, reassured my handgun was accessible. I anticipated other people in the house with Dan. I didn't know who or what else to expect.

I knocked on the front door, and I waited in the dark for someone to open it. The porch light flipped on. The door swung open. My eyes met Wolf's as Wolf answered the door. I had never met Wolf before, but I knew exactly who he was when I saw him standing in the doorway. I had heard some wild tales involving him. I wished he wasn't standing right in front of me.

"Wolf...is Dan here?"

Wolf already knew who I was, as well. He greeted me and shook my hand.

"Doug, come in. He's in the basement. Have a seat. Help yourself to food or drinks from the refrigerator if you wish. You're welcome to whatever you can find."

"I'm good. Thank you."

Wolf pulled out a chair in his kitchen. I took a seat. Wolf went down to the basement to find Dan. I sat there in the kitchen and wondered who else was in the house. A girl, someone I had never seen before, walked into the kitchen from the left side. She glanced at me as she hurried her way out of the kitchen, through the door on the other side of the room. I heard footsteps as people walked up from the basement. Wolf appeared first through the doorway. Dan was right behind him. I stood up.

Though I had only been away from Lansing for a brief time, it felt as if I hadn't seen Dan in years. It was as if he had aged a lifetime in the few short weeks I was gone. After our initial reunion, both of us took seats at the kitchen table. Wolf left the kitchen to go back to sleep in his bedroom.

"So...I've heard some things. I wanted to be sure you were

all right…"

I watched Dan. He began to explain what all happened in Lansing in my absence. I could tell he was stressed, a new stress I hadn't seen before. I could see he was paranoid. There was an air of desperation in his voice. There was worry. Dan was gravely concerned with his immediate future.

There had been violence in the city, with more expected. There had been a series of events which resulted in the death of an individual associated with an overlapping social circle. There had also been bulletins on the local news, reports that law enforcement sought Dan and a mutual friend for questioning in relation to a crime caught on surveillance video. Two completely separate situations, both weighed heavily on Dan that evening in Wolf's kitchen.

…

Luke was out of rehab and back in the streets of Lansing. Though I hadn't seen Luke since that night I first met Dan a year prior, Luke and I became inseparable after our reunion in spring of 2020. I helped Luke work on his car. He helped me work on mine. I tattooed him and some of his friends. I supplied him and his friends with fuel to party. He introduced me to a whole new circle of people in the Lansing underworld. I put Luke on, and I helped him level up.

"It's a go. He just texted me back."

"Bet. Let me get my stuff together, and I'll be ready to roll after I finish tattooing."

"All right. I'll let him know we'll leave here in about an hour."

"This should be fun. I haven't been to the Upper Peninsula since I was like twenty-five."

There were eight people sitting in Caleb and Simon's living room. I was at the dining room table. I had been tattooing my left arm for an hour. Occasionally, I took short breaks to do hotrails. Luke had been texting his friend, one who lived in the Upper Peninsula of Michigan.

I let Luke know I finally had a clear schedule that evening.

Luke previously informed his friend of the quality product I had at my disposal. His friend had been pestering him the prior week to take a trip to see him. Until that evening, I was too busy to make the trip. After I crunched some numbers, I relayed a dollar amount to Luke, one which was acceptable as a surcharge for the time, distance, and gasoline it would take to reach the Upper Peninsula and make it back to Lansing. Luke set up the transaction for that night.

Though my Lexus was running, and I had been driving fine around the lower regions of Michigan, I was still waiting for Dan to change out the exhaust system and catalytic converters. I bought the replacement parts, and I had them in my possession. The parts had been there since the previous stretch of time when I was in Lansing. I had been waiting on Dan to be around and available to do the work. He owed me a couple thousand dollars. The work on my car was a way to cut into that debt. Between hiding from the police, and whatever else Dan had been getting into, I couldn't wrangle him to do the repairs on my car.

After the hydroplaning incident the previous month, three of the tires on my Lexus had blown. The thought of driving my car to an unfamiliar and distant location wasn't sitting well. Though the three tires had been replaced, I wasn't sure the fourth tire would maintain integrity on a trip to the Upper Peninsula.

I rented an SUV for the evening trip. I needed to pick the car up from the rental agency at the Lansing airport. A friend dropped me off. With a handgun strapped around my ankle, and drugs in the backpack slung over my shoulder, I walked into the airport to sign paperwork and pick up the vehicle. I wasn't crossing through the terminal to any gates, so I didn't need to pass through any security checkpoints. I was handed the keys to the rental SUV. I left the airport and stopped back at Caleb and Simon's apartment to pick up Luke.

Peristalsis

I had been overhearing talk of two lists. I hadn't paid much attention when I caught random whispers in passing. The day came when I overheard multiple people, at various times and locations, mention those lists. I was sitting in a bedroom with Luke and five other people when I heard Luke tell one of his friends that the lists just came out. I asked Luke a question.

"What are you talking about a list, or lists? I've heard them mentioned before."

"I'll send them to you. Every so often, they put out two lists. One's a snitch list, and one's a hit list."

I didn't press the issue. A moment later, my phone beeped. Luke had sent me both of the newly released lists. I read the names on each of the lists. I remembered Dan, in his recent spiraling paranoia, had mentioned to me that he was worried he was on the hit list. I didn't see Dan's name anywhere.

I didn't recognize anyone's name on the snitch list. I was close with one person on the hit list. It was Ashley, the friend on the news story and surveillance video with Dan. Luke and his friend group had a rivalry with Ashley and Brittany. Something happened between them, positioning them as enemies. I stayed out of it, so I didn't know the specifics. I didn't want to know the specifics.

...

I sat on a couch in Jerry's living room and I noticed the clock. It was three in the afternoon. Ashley and two of her friends were in Jerry's kitchen making sandwiches. Dan and Jerry were near me, sitting on chairs in the living room. Two others were on another couch. I sat, and I listened to the people having random conversations around me. I was deeper in thought than I cared to express at the moment.

I wasn't paying specific attention to any one conversation. All the words from everyone in Jerry's house washed over me as I caught bits and pieces of different conversations. Dan stood up from his seat and headed to the kitchen. He stopped for a second in front of me.

"Are you alright, man? You're extra quiet..."

"I'm good. I'm just thinking."

Dan looked at me for another two seconds as he considered my response. He then nodded his head. He continued on his way to the kitchen. By three o'clock that afternoon, I had heard enough to put me in a weird headspace. Every person in the house that day was engaged in standard interactions with each other. I heard people discussing their plans for the upcoming week, plans for the near future, and plans for the summer, conversations I had heard many times before. The words, that day, held more weight than they had previously. There was something about the casual way everyone was discussing upcoming life...

I thought on it for another moment. It wasn't so much about everyone discussing upcoming life, it was the fact that life would go on unabated, and I wouldn't be there for any of it. Without saying a word to anyone, I stood up and walked outside to my car. I wasn't yet completely checked out of Lansing, but I was remarkably close...and I knew it.

...

Lee and I sat in my car in a parking lot in Howell, Michigan. My friend Lee worked a third shift job. The time came for him to leave and head to work. He had managed to compose himself over the previous hour, since he injected that large shot of crystal. Had I not talked him into doing just half of the amount he originally wanted to do, I figured he wouldn't have recovered at all.

Earlier in the evening, Lee tried to convince me that he had been doing shots of full grams of crystal. I flat out told him that he was either measuring wrong, injecting an extremely inferior product, or he was lying to me. I asked him to explain his process. I shook my head as soon as he told me how he measured the doses. I was genuinely annoyed when Lee explained his process. I had heard the same claim from others before.

"I crush up the crystal and fill the syringe all the way to the top line on the barrel. I use a syringe which holds a full cc, so each mark is a tenth of a…"

"Stop talking. How can you even think that's anywhere close to accurate? Those lines measure liquid. What if you crush the crystal more one time than another? What if you compress the powder more one time than another? What about the density of crystal? What does volume have to do with weight?"

Lee stared at me. He had no answers. He sat and thought to himself for another moment. I knew what he was about to say. I kept my mouth shut and waited for the inevitable next words to spill from his mouth.

"I'll do a gram of your stuff right now…"

"Again, stop talking. You absolutely won't do a gram of my stuff in a single shot. I'll properly weigh you out four tenths of a gram and prepare it correctly. I'll weigh it on a scale. I'll draw it up through cotton from a spoon. Four tenths will be enough to get you high beyond what you claim was a full gram shot."

It took Lee right up until he had to leave for work before he was able to articulate the errors of his previous technique. I made sure he knew the seriousness of being accurate when measuring drugs. Lee stepped from my car and walked across the parking lot to his parked car. I started my car, and I pulled from the parking lot.

There was a rest stop on I-96, just outside of Howell, Michigan. After Lee and I parted ways, I decided to stop off for some chill time and an ice cream sandwich. I was in the habit of frequenting rest stops while I traveled, and I knew that particular rest stop had the good ice cream sandwiches in the vending machine: strawberry ice cream in between two cookies.

I made it a point to stop at the rest stops I knew had the good ice cream sandwiches.

After an hour of sitting in my car, doing hotrails and interacting online, I decided it was time to leave the rest stop. I thought about it for a second and chose to step from my car to walk back into the service center for one more ice cream sandwich. I picked up my wallet from the center console and gathered up some loose trash from my front seats. I walked to the vending machine and bought the item of my desire. I then walked my bag of trash over to one of the garbage cans. I threw out my garbage and headed back across the parking lot to my car.

I left the rest stop. I planned to head to Ohio and sort through items in my storage unit for the remainder of the night. I planned to leave the storage complex in the morning. I was then going to spend the next three days in Fort Wayne, Indiana with a lady I had been interacting with online. She had a dominant personality, and we had discussed a fantasy which we planned to try together.

The sky was beginning to lighten the next morning as the sun was rising. I was sweaty and exhausted. For hours, I had been sorting, organizing, searching, and digging through all the items in my storage unit. Though the drugs kept me awake, I was physically drained. I decided to gather up the items for travel and take off for Indiana.

I pulled the storage unit's overhead door closed and organized my things in my car. I was hungry. I hadn't eaten anything since the ice cream sandwiches at the rest stop that prior night. I decided to order food and pick it up on my way out of Perrysburg. I reached toward the center console of my car to grab my wallet. It wasn't there.

A flash of panic washed over me as the memory of throwing away the bag of trash at the rest stop entered my mind. My wallet had been in my hand as I tossed the garbage in the can at the rest stop. I remembered it clearly. What I didn't remember was seeing my wallet at any point after I threw away the trash.

I combed my pockets. Nothing. I searched everywhere in

the front of my car. Nothing. My heart began to beat quicker. I postponed my plans to head directly to Indiana from Perrysburg. Over the next two hours, I removed every previously packed item from my car. I opened up my storage unit again, and I sorted through everything I had already sorted the night before.

I looked up information for the service center and found a phone number online. It was mid-morning at that point, and a rest stop attendant answered the phone when I called.

"Hi. I was there last night. I may have thrown away my wallet or dropped it in the parking lot…"

Moments passed. I waited with fingers crossed.

"Nobody here found anything."

My sense of panic grew inside me.

"Hey man, I'll be back there in the next two hours."

"Alright, I'll keep an eye out."

"Thank you." I hung up the phone. I forgot about being hungry.

I spent what was left of that morning, and early afternoon, at the rest stop. I looked everywhere I had been the prior night: the parking lot, the lobby, the bathroom. I waited until the night shift employees came to work at three o'clock that afternoon. They told me they hadn't found anything on their shift the previous night.

A week later, I finally headed to Fort Wayne, Indiana to stay with the lady I met online. A few hours after I left Lansing that Friday afternoon, I crossed over the border from Michigan to Indiana. I received a phone call from a number I didn't recognize as I approached my destination in Fort Wayne. Sometimes, I answered calls from unknown numbers…other times I didn't. I answered that phone call as I drove.

"This is Doug."

"Hi Doug. This is Officer Johnson of the Michigan State Police in Brighton, Michigan. We have…"

"No way," I interrupted the officer. "You guys found my wallet? Please tell me you found my wallet."

"We did," the officer answered.

"I can't believe it!"

I was thrilled. I hadn't cared that I had three hundred and fifty dollars in cash in the wallet. I had already cancelled my bank cards. My recovered drivers' license was what made me the happiest. It was two months into the coronavirus pandemic. Government offices and services were basically inaccessible. It was doubtful to downright hopeless to think I would have been able to procure a replacement drivers' license without extreme complications and delays...if at all.

"I had three bank cards, my New York apartment identification badge, my license, and three hundred and fifty dollars in cash in the wallet..."

"It's all still there."

"Dude...I'm in shock. Thank you so much. I'm out of town right now, but I'll be there after the weekend to pick it up. Thank you, for real. How'd you find it?"

"It was anonymously dropped off by a guy earlier today. He brought it in and left."

"Amazing. I'm shocked there are still other honest people out there. I'll see you on Monday. Much appreciated. Again... thank you."

"You're welcome. I'm happy we could help you out. See you Monday."

I thought about the whole situation. I had been seriously planning my exit from the scene up in Lansing. My drivers' license was crucial to making my exit. I spent that whole week not knowing how I was going to manage not having my license. I knew I had to leave Lansing. I knew how important it was to spend no more time than necessary in that toxic scene.

I breathed easier knowing I would soon have my license again. Had the police not called me, I would have had only bad thoughts of being stuck longer in Lansing. I breathed a sigh of relief. I grabbed my backpack as I stepped from my car, and I switched my focus to meeting that dominant woman, the lady with whom I was about to spend my weekend.

The drive back from Fort Wayne, Indiana was full of reflection. I thought of what had become of my life: my travel over the past couple of years, my consumption of crystal, my time in Lansing, and my sexual exploits. The dynamic that weekend, with a woman deep into the BDSM scene, had been enjoyable. Though I had been about that life, my body felt the results of the woman's desire to do things to me as she pleased. That feeling served to remind me that I had belonged to her over the previous couple of days.

I blew down one more hotrail as I exited the highway in Brighton, Michigan. I pulled into the police headquarters and parked my car. After about ten minutes inside the building, I walked back out to my car, reunited with my wallet and its contents. Again, I was amazed my wallet had even been recovered. I was more amazed that my license, bank card, and all the cash were still there in my wallet.

Since my bank cards had all been cancelled, I was then stuck waiting on my new cards to arrive by mail at my friend Jane's house in Ohio. I expected a phone call from Jane in the upcoming two weeks to let me know my new cards had shown up. Lansing was still my home base until I had my new bank cards.

I decided, right then, that I would leave Lansing for good as soon as I received those new bank cards. No exceptions. I felt happy with that decision. My days were numbered. I wasn't sure the exact day I would be gone, but at least I had an estimated time frame…a very short time frame.

Fast Years of Long, Slow Days

I reached Jerry's house in the late afternoon. Simon and Caleb's apartment had been my jump-off point in East Lansing after Dan no longer had his house. Jerry's house was my spot on the opposite side of the city. Though Dan was only around sporadically by May of 2020, I was most likely to run into him at Jerry's house.

I first met Jerry at Dan's house the previous year. Jerry was a gay guy in his mid-twenties. I didn't know how Dan knew Jerry. One morning in 2019, I woke up in Dan's living room, and Jerry was there. Jerry and I ended up in a lengthy conversation about how he needed to process and manage his feelings from his fiancé dying in a recent car accident.

Though I had no interest in anything sexual with Jerry, I could tell he was into me. I made it clear that the feeling was completely one-sided. He conceded the issue, but he also asked me for a favor. I listened to his proposal, and I told him that I was willing to help him out.

"Dan told me you're well-versed in the weird and the taboo. I've always had a fantasy I haven't tried."

"I can do that for you. I'll make it happen. I'm going to video it."

I told Jerry I'd be ready in thirty minutes. I told him I'd let him know when it was time. Jerry went into Dan's bedroom. I went to the kitchen and filled up an empty two-liter soda bottle with water from the sink. I drank half of it right away. I managed to drink the other half ten minutes later. Another ten more minutes, and I felt ready to go. I did all I could to hold off for yet another ten minutes. Finally, I could take it no longer. I knocked on Dan's bedroom door.

"Jerry let's go. I don't care if you keep your clothes on or not, but you need to get to the bathtub quickly. I can't wait any longer."

I set my phone on the windowsill in Dan's bathroom. Jerry stripped naked and got on his knees in the bathtub. Afterward, he thanked me for the experience. I zipped up and walked out of the bathroom without saying anything. Later, I sent Jerry a copy of the video. He replied with one word.

"Hot."

I continued to see Jerry periodically at Dan's house. Jerry and Dan made money streaming live videos on a social media platform. They had a makeshift studio in Dan's basement which they utilized to make content. When Dan lost his house, they moved the studio to Jerry's basement. Dan moved into Jerry's house.

When I arrived at Jerry's house on the evening I recovered my wallet, there was already a group of people there, friends and others I knew. They were all preparing food and setting up to have a cookout and bonfire that night. I settled in. Other people continued to arrive for the cookout at Jerry's house.

Though Ashley had her own business going on, due to the quality of my product, she was always a customer of mine for personal use. I sat with Dan, Ashley, and Brittany in an upstairs bedroom, hotrail after hotrail consumed off of my silver serving tray. While certain other people trickled in and out of the bedroom that evening, anyone I didn't know remained outside at the bonfire. I had no desire to interact with people I didn't know, and my friends were well aware.

…

I spent the following afternoon with Luke in a parking lot in Lansing, replacing a valve on the fuel line of Luke's car. We finished the repairs as the sky was almost dark and the mosquitoes were out in full effect. Both of us were sweaty and dirty from the work we had done. Luke told me to follow him in my car. We had a stop to make before we reached our next destination that night.

After we picked up what we needed to pick up, Luke and I each drove our own cars to the destination for the night. As I parked my car on the street behind Luke, he got out of his car and jumped into my passenger seat. Luke had also heard the gunshots as we were parking on the street. Two more shots rang out, and the two of us slumped lower in our seats.

Silence filled the air for a moment. Luke and I decided to stay in the car and stay low. Moments later, we heard police sirens approaching from behind us. I sat up after the lights and sirens passed by my car. I saw two police cars blaze around a corner two streets up from where I was parked, the area where the shots came from. The sirens cut off, but the red and blue flashing lights continued to reflect off of the houses two blocks in front of us.

Before we stepped from the car, Luke told me a story. He was convinced he had been given a hot shot by an associate the day before he entered rehab nine months prior. The hot shot was a syringe of heroin designed to cause him to overdose. Luke was sure someone wanted him out of the way.

"Who was with you that night?"

"Brad was there. I'm almost totally sure he knew ahead of time about the hot shot."

Luke and I both stepped from my car and walked up to the side door of Brad's house. His story echoed in my brain as we walked up to Brad's door. Though Luke was convinced there was nothing to worry about, I still wasn't fully comfortable knowing that Brad had known about it, the person who was supposed to be his best friend.

The story was just one of many examples of the scene in Lansing, Michigan; examples which I had either heard from others or witnessed myself. I knew I was close to being out of that scene forever, and I didn't want anything to come between me and that goal.

I had never seen the process before, but I knew what it meant to shake a bottle. I had never needed to be involved in any sort of manufacturing. I was also never in need of small quantities of crystal. I had sampled multiple friends' different personal supplies of shake and bake on occasions. Sometimes, the quality was surprisingly good. The chunky powder even approached the lower end of my exceptionally high standards for the large crystal rocks I always dealt with. I had also never seen the manufacturing process of those large crystal rocks. I was always on, but I was one step removed from the initial creation.

As I sat and watched Luke's friend shake a bottle, I did hotrails of my brand. Whether their final product would manage to register on my radar of quality didn't matter. I wasn't going to be there a few hours later to try it out. I had a trip to take that night to pick up more of what was guaranteed to be top tier. As I sat and watched the beginnings of what would get Luke and his friends high in my absence, I began to think about my routine of traveling around the country.

I shook off my daydreams of travel. My trip that night was business. Those trips were straight to the point. Rarely did I detour at all on those business trips, on those first legs to my destination. Return trips, once I re-upped, often involved many stop-offs to deliver.

As those in the house were lounging around, and while one of Luke's friends was hard at work manufacturing future drugs, I stood up and wished everyone a good night. I let Luke know I would be back the next day. I walked to the door to leave. As I stepped outside to the front yard, I heard footsteps behind me. I felt Jade's hand on my shoulder. My eyes met hers. I couldn't help but think, in that moment, how pretty her eyes were.

I had met Jade a couple of nights prior. Jade knew one of the guys in the house. When she showed up in the living room, seemingly out of nowhere, Luke and I were in awe of her oddly outgoing and bubbly personality. Jade was tall and beautiful. She had an undefinable quality about her. She didn't seem to fit in with the rest of the usual crowd. All the people in her presence seemed to vie for her attention.

Jade was drawn to me from the beginning, partly because I didn't fawn over her like everyone else. Gushing was never my style. Luke pulled me aside that first night to let me know how interestingly hot he found her. I agreed with him completely.

"Where are you going? Can I go with you?"

I thought about both of the questions Jade just asked me. I was lost in her beauty as we stood face-to-face. It may have been my weakness at that moment, but I already decided to let the scene unfold to its logical conclusion. I knew full well that I was breaking one of my cardinal rules when it came to my security involving the drug business...but I gave into the moment.

"I have to make a run. I won't be back until tomorrow..."

"I want to go with you."

"Alright...I'm leaving right now. Let's go."

On the way down South, Jade and I stopped off at my storage unit in Perrysburg. Jade was an impulsive person. She saw an electric hair trimmer in my storage unit. She told me she had thought about shaving the sides of her hair all the way around her head. Fifteen minutes after that, we both got back in my car; Jade had a new haircut. After the two of us shot crystal, I got back on track.

Jade and I were gone from Michigan for a full twenty-four hours. We stayed in a hotel, we had sex, we made some videos, and we stayed extremely high. On the return drive, I questioned my lapse in security for bringing someone along with me to a source. Later on, after returning to Lansing, I found out my worries were justified...but in a completely separate way than I had anticipated.

The ordeal which took place in Lansing in my absence that night was yet another dodged bullet, another confirmation it was time to leave that city for good. When Jade and I arrived back to Brad's house that next day, I could tell that something had happened in the time I had been away. Luke pulled me aside and told me what went down.

Luke told me a story about associates showing up and trapping out of Brad's house with them until they sold all their drugs, then the associates drugged and robbed Luke, Brad, and their friends. I looked around Brad's living room. The living room no longer had a television or a stereo. Luke, Brad, and a couple other friends no longer had their wallets, either.

Luke and his friends had been drugged and robbed. I too had been robbed in that same span of time. I realized it later that day, while at Caleb and Simon's apartment. I noticed one of the compartments of my bag was inexplicably empty. I thought back to a week prior.

...

MSM: Methylsulfonymethane $(CH_3)_2SO_2$...a supplement sold over the counter at drug stores. Luke and I walked the aisles of a pharmacy. Luke had me pick up a bottle of MSM.

"What, is your arthritis acting up?"

"There's another use for MSM. Trust me, you'll see."

After I spent a couple of hours at Brad's house with Luke, he dropped a bag into my lap.

"What's this?"

"It looks real, doesn't it?"

"Uh...yeah..."

"It's an ounce. It's yours for buying me that bottle of MSM."

"I don't want that. I have real drugs. I don't want fake drugs."

Luke, Brad, and their friends had a plan. They had been shorted money on a transaction a while back. They used MSM to make fake crystal. They set up a deal with the people who shorted them. They planned to sell the fake crystal to recover their losses. As always, I wanted no part in it. I gathered up my belongings. I had other places to be.

I put the fake ounce in my bag, in a separate compartment

from all of my legit ounces. I didn't know what I was going to do with it, but I was sure I would never sell it. I then forgot about it.

...

The main compartment of my bag was still full, filled with the weight I had just picked up, the exact amount I had just picked up. The smaller compartment, the zipper compartment with that single ounce-bag of fake MSM crystal that Luke had given me...it was empty.

During my time with Jade on the trip, she had robbed me. She managed to get an ounce from me, an ounce of crystal, the only fake ounce of crystal ever in my possession. I smiled. Jade had tried. All she had managed to accomplish was to rid me of a useless item, a novelty I was never going to use for anything. I called Luke to warn him to be wary of Jade, should he see her again in the future. She had sticky fingers.

I was still in Lansing. I wished to be anywhere else. I needed work done on the exhaust system on my Lexus. I needed to put pressure on Dan to do the work. The hourglass had been flipped over long ago, and the sand was running out. I didn't want to be there when those last grains of sand fell.

King of Wishful Thinking

I drove south from Michigan, into Ohio. After two more hours on the road, I reached my destination. I hated Lima, Ohio. It was my least favorite city in the state. I made an exception that day. I had been interacting online with an interesting couple. They wished to share intimacy with me. After a week of texting between the three of us, I made another exception: group sex.

Normally, I flat out declined offers from couples. The couple in Lima was different. Both husband and wife were very much in love after twenty years of marriage. I understood my role in their dynamic. I was there to enhance the intimacy between the two of them. I wasn't there to spice up their sex life, and I wasn't going to be a tool for one of them to invoke jealousy in the other. Both the man and the woman were looking for me to be an enhancement to their already healthy intimate dynamic.

The couple was different in another way as well. Though both of them appeared as husband and wife in their daily lives, their roles switched in the bedroom. The husband, masculine in his daily routine and interactions, became the female in bed. He wore lingerie and makeup, he wore a wig, and he adopted the mannerisms of a submissive female. The wife, as womanly as she was in her day-to-day, donned the role of dominant male in the bedroom. She tied up her hair, she wore the outfit of a blue-collar worker, and she was in charge. Though masculinity and femininity are independent of dominant and submissive roles, the couple lived a standard-role life outside of the bedroom.

I met the husband at the front door of the house. He offered me a glass of iced tea as he led me to the kitchen, where he introduced me to his wife. The couple had asked me what foods I liked to eat in a message the previous day. The two of them invited me to help them finish cooking. I set down my bag, and I helped them finish cooking the tacos they planned to have for dinner that evening.

The three of us talked about life as we ate the tacos. Interests, goals, hopes, dreams, we touched on multiple subjects. Their humor was pleasant. Their demeanor was kind and open. I felt welcome in their home. They discussed their lives, their children in college, their careers. I told them of my former career and of my current travels. I told them how I just left Lansing, Michigan, and how I looked forward to the adventures yet to come.

As we finished eating, our conversation switched to the subject of intimacy. The three of us cleaned up our dishes, and the couple invited me to join them in the bedroom. The wife took my hand and led me down a hallway. The husband followed behind us. We left the food on the island in the kitchen.

Three hours passed as the three of us shared intimacy in the couple's bedroom. At the wife's urging, I did things which the husband hadn't done before. I helped show them a new level of intimacy. The wife and the husband took turns watching as I interacted with the other. At times, all three of us engaged together. At one point, three hours into it, I became the one who watched as the spouses made love.

I took that moment as my cue. I told the couple I had worked up an appetite. I then went back to the kitchen to eat more tacos. I sat at their kitchen table and looked out the sliding glass door, into the backyard, as I ate more food. Twenty minutes passed while the husband and wife finished with each other in the bedroom. I finished eating as the two of them walked, smiling, into the kitchen to join me for more food.

I had been part of various intimate experiences involving multiple partners. Those experiences mostly fell short of satisfaction. In my mind, true intimacy always involved one hundred percent focus on a single person sharing the moment with me. Three or more people together always felt distracted, like too much was going on to fully appreciate other people sharing the moment. That time in Lima, Ohio became a rare exception; a couple, still very much in love with each other...still very much attracted to each other. A happy couple who invited me to share a small part of their love for each other.

I smiled as I bid them farewell, and I walked out the door. I was happy to share in that experience that day. I checked my phone when I reached my car. Tim had sent me the location of his hotel in Columbus. I set the address in my GPS, and I left my least favorite city in Ohio.

I decided to drive east before heading west. I took I-70 to Columbus, where Tim had been staying in a hotel. As I drove east on the interstate, my phone rang. I answered it. A recorded voice began reciting words.

"You have a collect call from the Shiawassee County..."

I hung up before I heard the remainder of the message from the jail up in Michigan. Dan was trying to reach me. Dan's lies and deceit had burned that bridge. Brittany previously told me of a wild night earlier in the week which landed Dan in jail. I was in no position to bail him out, even if he hadn't done what he had done over the prior few months. Since Dan had been lying to me the entire year, I had no desire to accept his phone call.

Before leaving Lansing, I found out Dan had lied to me continuously as he ran up a two-thousand-dollar tab for drugs. He went as far as to forge a letter from the IRS which stated his tax refund had a delay. That, after he had promised instant payback upon his receipt of the tax refund.

I called Dan out on his lies on an earlier phone call. He then admitted he already received, and spent, his tax return. He had strung me along for weeks. He took advantage of my trust in him. I no longer wished to help him.

I stuck my phone back to the velcro on my steering wheel.

I texted Tim. I told him to send me his room number. I was set to arrive in the Columbus area within the hour. Tim texted me the room number. I turned my attention back to the road for the remainder of the drive.

Tim had been staying at a Sheraton in Columbus for two weeks when I arrived there to see him. After I took a shower, I told him to text his plug. Due to coronavirus, the drug market had become unreliable. Though I weathered much of the storm, I had heard talk of entire regions inflating their prices...or running completely dry.

The pandemic affected some of my sources, so I decided to reach out to Tim. I didn't have a source in Columbus, Ohio... but Tim did. I agreed to the coronavirus mark-up, and we left to go meet Tim's guy in an apartment complex, a location which I had never before been. Tim left the car. I remained in the driver's seat. After a couple of tense minutes, Tim walked back over to my car and got in.

That meeting with Tim's guy was one of the last steps in my plan to vacate the Midwest. Tim and I spent the remainder of that night getting high in the hotel room. When I left the next morning, I told him that I would see him in about a week, when I passed through Columbus again on my way west. I planned to spend the week visiting friends in Pittsburgh and Philadelphia.

"I'll still be at the Sheraton. Hopefully, I'll be in an upgraded club-level suite by then."

'I look forward to the upgrade. I'll see you then."

...

Tim's wish had been granted when I arrived back in Columbus. While he moved his belongings to the new room on the top floor of the hotel, I wired a new amplifier into the trunk of my car, down in the hotel's parking lot. Tim came outside and handed me my new spare keycard. Our keycards not only worked to unlock the hotel room, but they also gave us access to a private club and dining area on the top floor of the hotel.

I was excited to explore the club level and suite in the hotel. The elevator only had buttons for eight of the floors of lodging. As Tim and I stepped into the elevator, the doors closed behind us. I scanned my keycard on the pad inside the elevator. A new floor number lit up on the screen. The elevator took us up to floor nine.

When Tim and I stepped from the elevator, nobody else was on the floor. We stopped at our suite so I could put my bags inside. I took a few minutes to survey the suite. There were two king-sized bedrooms, a living room area, an entertainment area, and two bathrooms in our hotel suite. The entertainment area came complete, with a fully stocked bar. It was a shame that neither Tim nor I drank alcohol, though the bar itself made a perfect setup to prepare crystal.

Tim's belongings were all in a bedroom on one side of the suite. I set my bags on the bed in the other bedroom on the opposite side of the unit. The two of us left the room to explore the exclusive floor of our hotel. As we walked the hallways, we realized we were the only people staying on the top floor. Tim scanned a keycard on the door to the club-level entertainment area.

The nightclub/entertainment area on that floor of the hotel looked like it was ready to host a banquet or a wedding reception. I recorded some videos in the empty luxury area. Tim and I wandered through the rooms. The two of us hung out in there for a bit. As the sun began to set that evening, we headed back to our suite to order food from the front desk. The two of us did drugs as we waited for our food to arrive at our door.

As we ate, I received a message from a woman who lived a few blocks from our hotel. She was a pretty African American lady who messaged me after she arrived home from work. She sought a no-strings-attached encounter that evening. I told her I would be over in twenty minutes. The lady told me to walk in, the door would be unlocked...she would be naked. I let Tim know I was stepping out for a short bit.

True to her word, the door to the apartment was unlocked. I walked into the lady's home. True to her word again, she was naked in her bed. She was beautiful. I had no reservations as I saw her, though I did have an issue. I had just injected a hefty dose of crystal right before I left the hotel suite. Though I was thoroughly aroused as the lady and I began to kiss, I knew I wasn't going to be able to perform.

The lady earlier expressed, in a text message, that she wanted me inside her. I told her I needed to make a compromise. I let her know that I wasn't going to fill her up that particular way. I also informed her of my prowess with my mouth. I guaranteed her satisfaction.

After about a half hour, my new friend enthusiastically confirmed I had gone beyond what she could have hoped. The lady wrapped herself in a bed sheet as I dressed. She walked me to the front door.

"When's the soonest you can come see me again?"

"Well, I'm about to head out West, probably tomorrow morning. I'm not sure when I'll be back in the Midwest, but I'll get a hold of you next time I'm back."

We kissed again before I walked out into the night. I drove the two blocks back to the hotel with a smile on my exhausted lips.

...

I was back in Lansing. A mix of unusual feelings swirled in my brain as I stepped from my car and into the early morning Lansing air. I had left Tim's club-level suite in the middle of the night. I had driven through the darkness of early morning and reached Lansing as the sun first began to evaporate the fog from the streets.

The pickup truck was still parked on the road across from the house. It had been sitting there for a few weeks. I previously stopped by the residence and recovered my car's air conditioning charging hose from the front seat of that pickup truck. On that instance, I noted at least three glass stems lying on the front bench seat. There was residue coating the insides of the pipes, residue from smoking methamphetamine.

The pickup truck belonged to a woman Dan knew. Though Dan was in jail, the pickup truck was still parked in the road. The girl who owned the truck still hadn't been able to locate it. Dan had used the truck to commit a crime, and the woman's truck remained there, where it sat since Dan was arrested at the house.

I knocked on the door and waited. I knocked again. The door opened and I stepped inside. I had been outside that particular house on multiple occasions. I had even hung out there before, just not inside the house. As the front door closed behind me, I noted to Brittany how it was odd that the truck was still sitting there on the street in front of her house. Brittany shrugged as we walked to her living room.

It was still morning as my final business in Lansing concluded. That particular business normally wouldn't have been worth taking the out-of-the-way drive. Since I always liked Brittany, I made the trip for her that day. I stepped back into my car and pulled from Brittany's driveway in the mid-morning.

It was an odd mix of feelings that morning. I felt relief, I was finally at the point of leaving. I felt sadness, despite the drama and stress. I knew I was going to miss many of the people in Lansing, Michigan. I felt nostalgic. I had many important moments and good times during the stretch of time with Lansing as my jump-off point for travel. I felt excited. The unknown and unexplored world beyond the Midwest was in my view.

My anxiety consumed me as I drove through the surface streets of Lansing. I knew I was literally moments away from leaving that chapter of my life behind. I felt it was the perfect time for catastrophe to impede my exit. All the work I did to separate myself from all the negative events which took place around me during that time…I hoped I could manage those last couple of miles in those last couple minutes, incident free… before my life could reset.

I reached the ramp to the interstate. I scanned the road in front of me. Hypervigilant, I checked my mirrors in all directions. I pushed my foot down, and the gas pedal of my Lexus sank to the floor. I blasted off. The crystal ran through my veins, it was overtaken by adrenaline. The anxiety washed through and out of me on that highway, and it stayed behind me in my past. My anxiety stayed in Lansing, Michigan.

Though I didn't have a clue what was to become of my life from that day on, I knew it would be like nothing I had experienced. The entire eastern half of the United States was, at that point, essentially my backyard. I knew it thoroughly. I could find my way anywhere based solely on recollection.

I had been to so many places so many times. The roads, the cities, the notable locations…the routes and alternate routes, the markers, the destinations…the best ways through cities and places based on traffic conditions or construction, the most scenic or leisurely paths, or the most time-efficient directions, the ways to avoid tolls, or reach out-of-the-way "secret" locations, I had mastered driving the entire eastern half of the country.

But out West, there were still nine states which I had yet to visit. I decided something right then; that trip, upon its completion, would end with forty-nine of the fifty United States holding memories of times I spent exploring them.

Phase Potentiation

On the weekend I moved out of my house in November of 2018, I dealt with a situation which complicated my move. There was a girl who took a bus to my house, all the way from Missouri. Her name was Dana. Dana and I shared a complicated four days together. I eventually managed to coax her onto a train which took her to Minnesota, where her family resided. I wasn't sure what had happened in Missouri to end Dana's stay there, but I was finally able to focus on moving out of my house once Dana was gone.

Dana and I had been in contact randomly since then. I hadn't been to Minnesota. I knew Dana was no longer staying with her mom in Saint Paul. She was staying in a college apartment with three other roommates in downtown Minneapolis. I called her as I drove through the city. She told me the name of the apartment where she lived. I called her again when I was in the apartment lobby. Dana met me by the front desk. She ran up to me and hugged me tightly.

I spent the week with Dana and her friends. She took me to her mom's house in Saint Paul, where I met various members of her family. I ended up tattooing her mom. The tattoo was of her girlfriend's name on the left side of her chest and was going to serve as a homecoming present when her girlfriend was released from prison a week later.

I stayed with Dana at the downtown college apartment in Minneapolis. Her roommates were gone, all back in their home cities on summer break from college. I stayed there with her, one of her friends, and her cousin.

Shortly after the four of us woke up one morning, one of Dana's roommates aggressively burst through the front door to the fifteenth-floor apartment. Suddenly, I was in the middle of a situation. I had no idea what was happening. The screaming quickly escalated to physical violence. I tried my best to stay between Dana and her roommate, but many of the punches got through. In the ensuing chaos, I managed to grab my belongings and remove Dana from the apartment, down the hallway, and into the elevator.

The fight resumed outside, fifteen floors below. In the courtyard outside the apartment building, security guards, Dana's friend, and I did all we could to keep the two ladies separated. A car screeched to a halt on the street by the courtyard. At the same time, Dana's cousin made it out into the courtyard. As the cousin ran up to join in the fight, two of the roommate's friends ran up from the car in the street. Bystanders tried to pull the fighting girls apart. Some of them absorbed punches from the ladies.

Sirens from a block over grew louder. Dana's friend and cousin took off for the cousin's car down the street. I pulled Dana into my car. I saw the police pull up in my mirror as they swarmed the courtyard, looking for the violence in the group of bystanders. I was almost certain all the girls involved in the actual altercation had managed to scatter before the police caught them.

Dana was still worked up as I drove from the scene. She was yelling and had tears in her eyes. Her clothes were ripped, spotted with blood, and streaked with dirt. I managed to calm her down. We stopped at a gas station outside the city. On the phone, Dana's cousin told her that they also made it safely from the scene. I planned to drop Dana off at her mom's place in Saint Paul. I realized something on that drive; I forgot my car jump starter battery pack in the apartment. I wasn't happy about it, but I conceded the loss.

I pulled into a rest stop in Saint Cloud, Minnesota as the

sun went down. It was nighttime. The rest stop was extremely crowded. The commercial truck lot was full, and overflow trucks were lining the ramps connecting the rest stop to the highway. Shady characters wandered around in the lot, between the many passenger vehicles which were posted up for the night. I put the shades up in the windows of my car, and I did drugs while I interacted with people on my phone. Eventually, I managed a few hours of sleep.

The next morning, I knew I had to address an issue with my car, one which was long overdue. I drove through Saint Cloud. It was the Fourth of July. I managed to find an open auto supply store and bought new front brakes, rotors, and the correct brake fluid. I found an appropriate parking lot around mid-afternoon. The lot was empty except for the cars up front near the Walmart entrance. I parked along the side of the building, as far across from the pharmacy as I could. I then began to gather up the needed tools.

The next hours, into the dark of night, I changed the brakes and the rotor for the driver's side wheel. I could see the flashing of fireworks in the distance on the horizon. I could hear fireworks as they echoed from multiple directions sporadically throughout the evening. I completed the work on my car as the holiday concluded. I was dirty, soaked in sweat, and bit up by mosquitos. I was hot, dehydrated, and exhausted.

The sunrise was breathtaking as I drove on the interstate the next morning. I set up my phone to record video as I drove west in Minnesota. My chemical enhancement had fueled the drive through the night. As the sun rose, so did my mental state. I felt a twinge of excitement knowing I was about to check more states off of my list. I had loose plans with people all over the western half of the country. Though I left the substance market behind, I still had a decent quantity of crystal along with me for the ride. I knew that once I left Minnesota, the true adventure was set to begin.

...

It was hot and sunny when I crossed from Minnesota to

Fargo, North Dakota. I drove through the city until I found a rest stop. I gathered up my drugs, a towel, body wash, and a clean set of clothing. I went inside and paid for a shower. The rest stop was crowded, so I waited in the lounge area until my number was called. I walked down the hallway until I found the appropriate room number. Once inside, I locked the door. I stripped and set up my drug tray. I did a hotrail and placed my phone so I could video-call with a lady from the internet as I showered.

Truck stop/travel center showers were always enjoyable experiences. The rooms were usually quite spacious. There was a sink area, a toilet area, a bench to sit on, racks to hang clothes and towels, and a tile shower area. Rest stop showers were perfect spots to take breaks from driving, get clean, do drugs, use the facilities, and video-interact with others in privacy.

Forty-five minutes later, I was back outside at my car. I was pouring sweat again as soon as I stepped outside the service center. I decided to spend the day in Fargo working on more of my car audio system. Between my meth consumption and my compulsive purchases of stereo components, the work was never done. I traveled with all the needed tools in my car. Anywhere became a good spot to add more sound to my Lexus.

Hours later, I was driving on the interstate, heading south in the Dakotas. I was going to be passing through Sioux Falls, South Dakota later on that day. I had been messaging back-and-forth with an Asian lady who was a resident there. According to her, she was recently divorced, and she had moved into a hotel room with her dog and all her belongings. She wanted me to stop to see her on my way through the city. I agreed. The lady sent me an address, and I replied to her with the ETA.

I knocked on the door to the hotel room. The lady opened the door and led me inside by my hand. She then kissed me and told me to get comfortable on the bed. She went into the bathroom and shut the door. I sat back against the headboard and took note of the many racks of hanging clothes filling up the far side of the room. The lady's elderly dog lay on the floor in a dog bed over by the window. Twenty minutes passed, and I walked to the bathroom door and knocked.

"Are you okay?"

"I'm fine."

I sat back down. Ten more minutes passed. The lady finally stepped out of the bathroom. She told me to come outside with her as she walked her dog.

"I'm going to smoke a cigarette while we're out here."

"Aright. I'm gonna run to my car quick."

Once in my car, I put the shades up in my windows. I injected crystal into my arm. I sat for a bit while the drugs hit and washed over me. I sat a bit longer. Another ten minutes passed. I wasn't going to go back to the lady's hotel room. She hadn't texted me to come back inside, and I hadn't texted her to say I wasn't coming back. I pushed the button to start my car, and I left Sioux Falls, South Dakota.

It was a long drive through the Dakotas, two more states crossed off the list. I reached Sioux City, Iowa and began receiving online notifications from interested people on the border of Iowa and Nebraska. It was early morning. The sun hadn't yet risen. I opened a message from a guy who had just finished his shift at the slaughterhouse in South Sioux City, Nebraska. I told him I would be at his house by seven o'clock that morning. That meant I had only an hour before I could cross yet another state off of my travel list.

The morning sky was beginning to brighten that Friday when I reached Cliff's house, one block from the slaughterhouse where he worked the third shift. Cliff was off work for the weekend. He partied. He had a bag of his own when I showed up. He wanted me to try it. Cliff loaded an oil-burner stem. I hit the pipe and shook my head as I blew out a cloud. It tasted impure compared to the ounce I had in my pocket. I flicked a crystal to Cliff.

"Try that."

As Cliff blew out his cloud of smoke, he was instantly

animated and hyper. He had never smoked anything close to what I had with me. Cliff wanted to buy half an ounce from me.

"I'm out of the game, dude. All I have is for personal use. The best I can do is a teener. It's gonna be expensive."

Cliff happily paid an exorbitant rate for a sixteenth of an ounce. Between making videos and doing drugs, Cliff took me around the city. We went to eat at a few local favorite restaurants. We got groceries at the store to grill out in Cliff's backyard. At one point, Cliff went to a cookout at his sister's house. During that time, I went to meet up with someone who had found me on one of the apps.

I left Cliff's house in South Sioux City, Nebraska. I wasn't able to set a goal to cross to the next state by the end of the same day. Nebraska was just too large. I faced the situation and drove. As hours passed, I kept plugging along. The low rolling hills and farmland were perpetual peripheral scenery. The sun shone bright to the green and golden-brown land of Nebraska as I kept on driving west.

Morning passed into afternoon. Afternoon became evening. The hours grew difficult when the evening sun was directly in front of me. Later on, as evening gave way to night, I was able to see again as I drove, the sun no longer shining through my front windshield. The traffic on the Nebraska highway was minimal, a clear vision in front of me. I had a long way to drive to reach the other side of the state. I blew down a hotrail and decided to spike my adrenaline.

I seized the opportunity. I thought back to the times on the interstates around Detroit, my own personal speedway. I cranked up the music. The bass vibrated my mirrors and my seat. I felt each note reverberate through my entire body. I gripped the steering wheel in front of me, and I pushed down on the gas.

The fields on either side of the road began to pass by more quickly. My focus, fueled by the drugs, cleared. As the needle on my speedometer crossed over into triple digits, a smile crept onto my face. My foot pushed further down to the floor. I felt the power of my Lexus's engine. One twenty...one thirty...one thirty-five...I was floating.

Over the next couple of hours, I balanced my legal speed-limit driving with bursts and extended stretches of pushing one hundred and forty miles-per-hour. I wasn't going to reach the next state that particular day, but I was going to find out how close I could get.

I eventually pulled into a rest stop off the highway. I set up for the night in my car at that rest stop, next to the highway in western Nebraska. The weather changed as I did hotrails and interacted online. The wind picked up almost instantly at one point. The air felt different. I removed the shade from my driver's side window. In the distance west of me, over the trees outlining the parking lot, lightning lit up the sky. It wasn't just a little lightning; it was nonstop. The sky was lit more than it was dark. Flashes overlapped and outshined previous bursts. I'd never seen anything like it. I recorded a video from outside my car for a short moment...and then the rain began. It was sporadic at first. I knew something bad was about to happen.

I stepped back in my car and closed up the window with the shade. I went online to check for news bulletins. I figured out my location, and I checked the internet. I pulled up radar of the sky. My eyes opened wide. I found a warning from the National Weather Service.

Growing up in the Midwest, tornado warnings and severe storm warnings were common. I wanted to be a storm chaser back when I was a child. I studied weather. I saw my first tornado when I was twelve years old. I loved severe weather, and I was always someone who chose to run towards a storm when there was a warning to take shelter.

The storm that night in Nebraska was different. I didn't have an option to shelter. My car was my home. The warning from the National Weather Service was like no other I had ever seen. The warning wasn't written as an option or a suggestion. It was urgent, to the point, and serious.

"Eighty-five mile an hour wind gusts, baseball sized hail, torrential rains…destruction. Immediately, no exceptions, take cover. People and animals outside WILL be hurt…or worse."

Then came the sound. I heard it start at the far west side of the parking lot. I was parked in the northeast corner. The sound grew louder as the storm pushed closer. It wasn't a tornado. It was wind-driven rain and hail. The wind hit my car in bursts as I felt the car's frame swaying on the suspension. I took the shade out of the passenger window. Sheets of water blotted out the giant lights on telephone poles throughout the parking lot… then, all the lights cut off. The sound of the rain and hail was as loud as the darkness was black. I was in it, and I made a choice in that moment.

I turned on my car, and I very slowly drove back to the highway. I felt I was safer on the road, no longer waiting for a tree to fall on my car. The drive was slow as the rain came down, unrelenting. After an hour, I made it to the next rest stop. I hadn't slept in days. I could barely see the road in front of me. I pulled into that next rest stop, and I slept in my car.

When I was awakened by noises the next morning, I saw the sunlight shining through the edges of the shades in my car windows. I pulled down the corner of the shade on my windshield. My jaw dropped. The noises had been coming from a crew of workers using power saws and woodchippers all around me in the parking lot.

More than half of the trees at the rest stop had snapped at their trunks and lay in the parking lot on the ground. A mature maple tree had fallen and filled the parking space two spaces down from where I had fallen asleep in my car. Trees were down behind me, in front of me, and on both sides. I recorded another video. I fixed the shade to cover the windshield once more. I did a hotrail. I was naked already, so I took the time to video-call an online friend.

I dressed and removed the shades from all my car's windows. The workers were still sawing away at the branches of the felled trees. I dodged the branches and trees which littered the pavement as I made my way back to the highway. It was a new day, sunny and cloudless. I was able to set a goal to reach the border of Nebraska that day. I was only a few hours away from crossing over into Colorado for the first time in my life. I was excited...and I blew down another hotrail to celebrate. I picked up speed, traveling west on the interstate.

The Golden State...I saw it, beginning in western Nebraska. The rolling hills of western Nebraska were a uniform color of golden beauty. I was an hour out, and I exited the highway to get food and gas. It was noon. I had been driving all morning. The downed trees at the rest stop were hours behind me in my rearview mirror. Anticipation tingled in my brain, enhanced from the crystal.

As I crossed the Nebraska/Colorado border, I felt my eyes begin to mist up. I saw the world's beauty all around me. I was in a moment, a golden moment, accentuated by the color of the land. I was significant, if only to myself. I was a passenger on a journey beyond that which I saw through my windshield.

It was an unfamiliar environment to me, and I loved the new life experience. I knew that I was exactly where I was meant to be. All the choices which led me to that exact location in that specific moment in time, all the options I didn't take... everything; it was the feeling I had been chasing for as long as I could remember. I was living life. I felt it; I felt alive. I felt like a person...a person connected to the entire world around me.

The past was behind me, the future was unknown, life made sense. I did up a hotrail as excitement filled my head. The possibilities were suddenly immeasurable. I felt whole. I was full inside. My last words to my mom were finally true, if only for that fleeting moment. Though homeless and alone, with no income and no idea of what was to come, and without any semblance of a normal or stable existence, I was okay...

www.ingramcontent.com/pod-product-compliance
Lightning Source LLC
Chambersburg PA
CBHW060823050426
42453CB00008B/557